SEVEN
LEVELS OF
PROMISE
For The OVERCOMER

The Book of Revelation Is Relevant

ARTHUR L. MACKEY JR.

SEVEN
LEVELS OF PROMISE
FOR THE OVERCOMER
The Book of Revelation Is Relevant

ARTHUR L. MACKEY JR.

Mackey Productions
Catch The Vision of Victory & Never Give Up

7 Levels of Promise for the Overcomer – The Book of Revelation Is Relevant
by Arthur L Mackey Jr.

Printed in the United States of America

ISBN: 978-0-615-19077-8

TABLE OF CONTENTS

DEDICATION

Seven Levels of Promise for the Overcomer: The Book of Revelation Is Relevant is dedicated in loving memory of my uncle, Trustee Walter R. Mackey, Jr., and my aunt, Mrs. Inez Dennis. Losing the both of you back to back in the summer of 2007 was hard. As the songs say, we will "See you in the rapture some great day", and "At the meeting around throne".

Revelation 14:13

*"And I heard a voice from heaven saying unto me, Write, Blessed are the dead which die in the Lord from henceforth: Yea, saith the Spirit, that they may rest from their labours; and their **works** do **follow them**."*

ACKNOWLEDGEMENTS

I would like to take this opportunity to say, thank you, to seven special people who, by the grace of God, helped make the God-given vision for this book a reality. Special thanks to my wife, Brenda, and my children, Yolanda, Jordan, and Faith, for your patience as I wrote and rewrote this book over the last seven years.

To Myrna Games, thank you for helping pull this project together in its infancy stage.

To Stephen W. Nance, thank you for being the great editor that you are. To Elder Vivian Mackey Johnson, (who has been with Mackey Productions since its inception), thank you for designing the cover, and for helping in the graphic design and proofreading. Thank you also to the staff at Fresh Eyes for doing a great job on the final edit.

PREFACE

Jesus Christ - the Overcomer,

Is the Founder of the Civil Rights

Movement

✝ **Revelation 7:9**

*"After this I looked and there before me was a great multitude that no one could count, from **every nation, tribe, people and language**, standing before the throne and in front of the Lamb. They were wearing white robes and were holding palm branches in their hands."*

Jesus Christ, the ultimate Overcomer, is the true Founder of the Civil Rights Movement. It is only because of the finished redemptive work of Jesus Christ on Calvary's old rugged cross, that every **nation,** and thus, every ethnic group known to humankind will be represented before the Throne and in front of the Lamb. Now please remember the extremely famous phrase in the Lord's Prayer which states in Matthew 6:10, *"Thy kingdom come, Thy will be done in earth, as it is in heaven."* If

Jesus Christ desires His Father's will to be done in earth, as it is in Heaven, **then it is God's perfect will for ethnic equality to exist on earth, because it certainly exists in Heaven. The theology of equality, as expressed and manifested through the ministry of Jesus Christ, is the very foundation of the true Civil Rights Movement.**

Revelation 7:9 makes it crystal clear that in Heaven there will be *"a great multitude that no one could count, **from every nation, tribe, people and language**, standing before the throne and in front of the Lamb."* The Greek word for nation is *ethnos* from which we get our English word *ethnic*. Therefore, Jesus also desires every ethnic group, nation, tribe, people, and language, to be totally transformed by His love down here on earth. John 3:16, which states: *"For God so loved the world, that he gave his only begotten Son, that whosoever believeth in him should not perish, but have everlasting life"*—the most famous verse in the entire Bible, is classic living proof of this concept of God's love which also indirectly gives birth to the concepts of civil and human rights since humankind, *"whosoever", i*s made in the image of the living and loving God.

In their thought provoking book entitled: *Black Man's Religion–Can Christianity Be Afrocentric?* Pastor Glenn Usry and Hood Theological Seminary New Testament professor, Craig S. Keener, have an outstanding chapter entitled: "God of Our Weary Years: Identification on the Basis of Common Oppression" in which they state concerning Revelation 7:9, "We hope for a better vision of racial and cultural diversity, where allegiance to a God who created all peoples in his image provides appreciation of rather than distaste for diversity. This is the vision of hope portrayed in Revelation 7:9: *"After these things I looked, and behold a great crowd which no one could count, from every people and tribe and language, standing before God's throne and before the Lamb..."* Revelation warns of a perverse unity among peoples for the purposes of evil in this world (13:7-8, 16) but promises that those who share God's kingdom will also share in the ultimate expression of multicultural diversity in unity before God's throne."[1]

Seven Scriptural Reasons Why Jesus Christ is the True Founder of the Civil Rights Movement

1. When a woman was caught in the very act of adultery (John 8:3-11). Jesus did not allow her bloodthirsty accusers—a deeply religious mob fully armed with legal arguments from the Law of Moses—to discriminate against her nor to kill her. Jesus, the Founder of the Civil Rights Movement, wrote in the sand and then declared in John 8:7: *"He that is without sin among you, let him first cast a stone at her."* The modern day Civil Rights Movement has to stop the stone casters who want to crush and kill people instead of helping hurting people come to a place of healing and wholeness. From the youngest to the oldest, each of the women's accusers

---

[1] Glenn Usry & Craig S. Keener, Black Man's Religion – Can Christianity Be Afrocentric?, Inter Varsity Press, Downers Grove, Illinois, pg 110

walked away. Jesus told the woman caught in the act of adultery in John 8:11 "Neither do I condemn thee: go, and sin no more." **Jesus Christ liberated and totally transformed this women's life forever.**

2. When a mega crowd of 5000 men, (many with their wives, mothers, grandmothers, sisters, aunts, and children, as well), were hungry, Jesus, the Founder of the Civil Rights Movement, was given a little boy's lunch which consisted of two fish and five loaves of bread. Jesus blessed it and brake the bread. After that, He had the disciples to sit the people down in groups of 50, which probably totaled to more than 15,000 when you average in the women, and children who were there. Jesus fed them all having twelve baskets filled to the brim with leftovers. **Jesus Christ started the concept of feeding the hungry which has led to modern day food pantries, soup kitchens, and other feeding outreaches both locally and worldwide.**

3. When the disciples of Jesus wanted conveniently to discriminate against children, Jesus Christ said in Luke

18:16: *"Suffer little children to come unto me, and forbid them not: for of such is the kingdom of God."* **Jesus Christ led the fight for the Human Rights of little children who are daily discriminated against throughout the world.**

4. Jesus did not discriminate against women. In fact, women were the very first witnesses to His resurrection. The women literally saw the two angels in the empty tomb who told the women in Luke 24:6: *"He is not here, but is risen."* This decision from the Godhead, the Father, Son, and Holy Ghost, to have women as the very first witnesses to testify to the apostles concerning the resurrection of Jesus Christ, was and is a clear example and firm stand against sexism. Luke 24:10 clearly shows this: *"It was Mary Magdalene and Joanna, and Mary the mother of James, and other women that were with them, which told these things unto the apostles."* **The revelation of Jesus Christ clearly declares that God is an equal opportunity employer.**

5. Jesus Christ clearly healed hurting people, such as the crippled, lame, lepers, and even a blind man on the Sabbath day, which was a clear act of civil and religious disobedience. John 9:14 declares: *"And it was the Sabbath day when Jesus made the clay, and opened his eyes."* These very acts of miraculous healing by Jesus Christ were the very impetus for modern day hospitals and medical care. Many religious leaders of Jesus' day literally hated Him, because He healed the hurting and opened the eyes of the blind on the Sabbath, thereby breaking the law. St. Augustine went on to write years later: "An unjust law is no law at all." **Both the concepts of effective medical care and civil disobedience all have their very roots in the ministry of Jesus Christ.**

6. Jesus Christ deeply cared not only in word, but also in deed, for the lame, the lepers, and hurting people who longed daily for health and wholeness. When John the Baptist was in prison and about to be beheaded, Jesus sent these very words to him as recorded in **Matthew 11:5**: *"The blind receive their sight, and the lame walk, the lepers are cleansed, and the deaf hear, the dead are* *raised up, and the poor have the gospel preached to them."* Jesus Christ led by example by carrying His own cross. Since Jesus was and is God, He could have stopped the Roman soldiers right in their tracks. The bloody march that Jesus led to Calvary pulled in a Black man, named Simon of Cyrene to help bear His cross. Mark 15:21 declares: *"And they compel one Simon a Cyrenian, who passed by, coming out of the country, the father of Alexander and Rufus, to bear his cross."* **The direct historic connection between Jesus carrying His own cross, and then a Black Jew, Simon of Cyrene, bearing His cross, brings about the connection of black men and women, slaves and descendents of slaves, like Frederick Douglass, Harriet Tubman, Martin Luther King Jr, and many others who boldly bore the cross of Jesus Christ to bring "whosoever" believeth into true freedom.**

7. In Matthew 25:34-40 Jesus Christ lets us know that the person who inherits the Kingdom is going to be the true godly person who feeds the hungry, helps the stranger,

clothes the naked, and visits the prisoner for the right reason. *"Then shall the King say unto them on his right hand, Come, ye blessed of my Father, inherit the kingdom prepared for you from the foundation of the world: For I was an hungred, and ye gave me meat: I was thirsty, and ye gave me drink: I was a stranger, and ye took me in: Naked, and ye clothed me: I was sick, and ye visited me: I was in prison, and ye came unto me. Then shall the righteous answer him, saying, Lord, when saw we thee an hungred, and fed thee? or thirsty, and gave thee drink? When saw we thee a stranger, and took thee in? or naked, and clothed thee? Or when saw we thee sick, or in prison, and came unto thee? And the King shall answer and say unto them, Verily I say unto you, Inasmuch as ye have done it unto one of the least of these my brethren, ye have done it unto me."* **If Jesus Christ of Nazareth was never born in Bethlehem of Judea there would never have been a Civil Rights Movement, because only the Creator of all humanity can teach humanity what true Civil and Human Rights is all about.** The revelation is relevant. We shall overcome.

Since Jesus Christ is the founding leader of a divinely ordained movement of equality then Christians should be concerned about healing the sick, feeding the hungry, clothing the naked, rescuing the perishing, and caring for the dying just like Jesus.

Notes For The Overcomer

INTRODUCTION

Wake Up!–The Condition and The Position

The timeless truth of the classic Book of Revelation introduces the blood-washed believer to Jesus Christ's clarion call to bring content back into the very heart and soul of Christianity. *Seven Levels of Promise for the Overcomer – The Book of Revelation Is Relevant* was written with the purpose in mind to clearly point the modern-day church back into the everlasting arms of the Ultimate Overcomer, Jesus Christ, and to end a longstanding love affair with the spirit of compromise, and to finally stop an ongoing spiritual fling with an utterly weak, lazy, shallow-minded, and completely carnal misrepresentation of Christianity.

My approach to this issue is to reveal the importance of the number *seven* in the Book of Revelation. Throughout the Bible, in the human body, in human history, in the earth, in the sea, and on the land—the number seven has been a clear expression of God's hand in all of creation. The theme throughout is that the revelation is relevant. Along the way, I show the tremendous impact of the Book of Revelation on the writing of old Negro spirituals and as inspiration for the Civil Rights movement. If people coming out of slavery were inspired to greatness by the Book of Revelation, then readers, warriors, workers, worshippers, writers, and rappers should also discover and delight in its modern-day relevance. My prayer is that the contents of this book will not only help bring much needed content back into Christianity, but also bring meaningful Christ-centered content back into modern day culture.

Whether it is an inter-racial worship and praise team singing the position, "We Have Overcome," or veteran Civil Rights leaders marching and boldly singing the condition, "We Shall Overcome," the Book of Revelation backs up both statements. The position and the condition are both biblically sound, therefore everyone can be on the same page and not in different little camps. The anthem "We Shall Overcome," which speaks to our current earthly, economic, social, and political condition as a persecuted people, is correct because Revelation chapters two and three refer distinctly, seven times, to the person "that overcometh." In terms of the earthly condition, we have not all arrived. Deep-seated racism, sexism, anti-Semitism, and pure hatred still exist all over the earth, but "We Shall Overcome".

The revelation is relevant for this very hour. The "We Have Overcome" worship and praise theme speaks clearly and directly to our position as blood-washed believers in Christ, for Revelation 12:11 boldly declares: *"And they overcame him by the blood of the Lamb, and by the word of their testimony; and they loved not their lives unto the death."*

"We Shall Overcome" – the Christian's condition, and "We Have Overcome" – the Christian's position, are both biblically sound statements of pure Christ-centered faith. One should never be used against the other. Praise and protest must work hand in hand. The worshiper and the warrior must operate together. Too many Christians today want to totally ignore the condition and only declare the position. You have to feel the pain and plight of the Christians and non-Christian's "We Shall Overcome" condition in order to appreciate the tremendous power of the Christian's "We Have Overcome" position.

Wake Up! The system of racial hatred, the system of the antichrist, the system of bigotry, racism, sexism, and anti-Semitism is alive and well. My grandfather, the late Rev. Walter R. Mackey, Sr., left Georgia and came to New York many years ago, because the Ku Klux Klan was trying to lynch him with their hatred and hangman's noose.

Wake Up! In September 2006, three nooses, clear symbols of racial hatred, were found hanging from the tree on the grounds of Jena High School in Jena, Louisiana. Rosa Parks, the Mother of Civil Rights Movement, hit the nail right on the head when she said "Racism is still with us. But it is up to us to prepare our children for what they have to meet, and, hopefully, we shall overcome."[2]

Wake Up! A noose was found hanging from an African-American Columbia University professor's door. In October 2007, two nooses were found hanging from a forklift in the garage at the Town of Hempstead Highway Department Yard in my hometown of Roosevelt, New York, and on January 10, 2008, a marker drawing of a noose was discovered on the locker of an African-American worker in the Town of Hempstead Department of Sanitation in Merrick, New York.

Wake Up! A Nassau County Department of Public Works employee found an 18-inch noose at a public works garage in Baldwin. Tara Todd, youngest daughter of Minister-in-training,

---

[2] Rosa Parks, The Mother of the Civil Rights Movement, concerning preparing our children to overcome.

Constance Todd, works at one of the sites where a noose was found most recently. Minister-in-training, Todd, herself, remembers seeing her very own Uncle Jimmy with a dirty old noose around his neck, hanging from a tree in Demopolis, Alabama, when she was only six years old. She has vivid memories of seeing many Black men and women hanging from trees while growing up in Birmingham, Alabama. In particular, she remembers that many Blacks were lynched when Rev. Dr. Martin Luther King, Jr. was imprisoned in Birmingham, where he wrote his now famous *Letter From Birmingham Jail* in 1963. It was for this very reason that King said in a 1962 speech at Cornell College: "It may be true that the law cannot make a man love me, but it can keep him from lynching me, and I think that's pretty important."[3]

Wake Up! Bull Connor, the racist Public Safety Commissioner of Birmingham, Alabama, may be dead, but his anti-Christian activities are being lived out daily by modern day, poorly trained police officers who only shoot to kill, and not to wound or stop, and then discover that their victim only

---

[3] Rev. Dr. Martin Luther King, Jr. Speaking against lynchings, Cornell College, Mount Vernon, Iowa Reported in the Wall Street Journal, November 13, 1962

had a hairbrush or a bag and not a gun. Dr. King was right when he wrote in his *Letter From Birmingham Jail* that "Injustice anywhere is a threat to justice everywhere".[4]

Black on Black crime is going on as well, and antichrist racists love it. A man who should be protecting the women of his local community climbs through an open window and rapes a precious young woman. Grown men who should be protecting the senior citizens of the local community climbed in through an open window, held a gun to a precious senior mother's face (whose son fights daily to improve the community), and robbed her house before her son got home.

Wake Up! Gang members are killing people in broad day light as well as during the night. Whether it is the Arian Nation, Ku Klux Klan, the Bloods, the Crips, or the ignorant fellow who robs and rapes in his very own community, it is all the system or spirit of antichrist—evil that speaks the Lordship of Christ merely with their mouth only, but utterly and daily deny the true deity of Christ through their evil actions. Burning a cross, hanging a noose, painting a swastika, conducting a drive-by shooting, raping the women we were created to protect,

---

[4] Letter From Birmingham Jail, Rev. Dr. Martin Luther King, Jr., April 16, 1963, The Estate of Martin Luther King, Jr.

robbing the senior citizens who were created for us to care for, all of these are antichrist acts of hatred which spit total disregard, dishonor, and disrespect on the true finished work of Christ. These acts of hatred deny the Father and the Son. If Jesus is truly Christ in our life, then He must be Christ enough to help us love one another.

William Seymour

Wake Up! In 2006 we celebrated the 100th anniversary of the great Azusa Street Revival, led by a Black preacher, William Seymour, whom the Lord used mightily in the early 1900's to bring the races together under one roof in true worship that revolutionized the world. In 2009 we will celebrate the 100th anniversary of the National Association for the Advancement of Colored People (NAACP), an organization that has faithfully led the good fight of faith in the courts and on the streets, throughout the years, against lynchings and racial discrimination, and for equal rights, jobs, and housing. We must not allow the nation to go back to the dark ages of an anti-Christian, racist, lynch mob mentality.

Here is what the Word of God has to say about such anti-christ activities and people:

✟ **1 John 2:22:**

"Who is a liar but he that denieth that Jesus is the Christ? He is antichrist, that denieth the Father and the Son."

✟ **1 John 4:3:**

"And every spirit that confesseth not that Jesus Christ is come in the flesh is not of God: and this is that spirit of antichrist, whereof ye have heard that it should come; and even now already is it in the world."

✟ **2 John 7:**

"For many deceivers are entered into the world, who confess not that Jesus Christ is come in the flesh. This is a deceiver and an antichrist."

God has called us to maturity and to overcome this evil system of Satan, the spirit of the anti-christ, by the blood of the Lamb and the word of our testimony. Dr. King said:

"We...have come to this hallowed spot to remind America of the fierce urgency of now."[5] Yes, today, we must remind America and all of the nations of the earth of the "fierce urgency of now". Now is the time to heed the call of Christ to be overcomers, and thereby in the process of living out the true essence of the songs, "We Shall Overcome" and "We Have Overcome," bring meaningful content back into the very heart and soul of Christianity and modern day culture.

---

[5] Rev. Dr. Martin Luther King, Jr., March on Washington Speech, Lincoln Memorial, Washington, D.C., August 28, 1963

Notes For The Overcomer

CHAPTER ONE

The Revelation is Relevant

The Revelation was and is relevant, and this is obvious, even before we study in detail the seven churches of Asia Minor, the seven seals, the seven trumpets, the seven significant signs, the seven vials, the seven significant scenes, and the seven sights of consummation in the Book of Revelation.

The relevant revelation of seven literally represents God's very own fingerprint and DNA in all of His awesome creation. The relevant revelation of seven literally drives an extremely sharp stake right through the very heart of the deadly "So what?" mentality. The relevant revelation of seven is the actual living proof that Charles Darwin's theory of evolution was and is totally wrong. Man did not evolve from monkeys. God created man in His own image, and seven is His number of completion. God created man on the sixth day of creation, and on the seventh day He rested. Scripture is quite clear on this, as the following passages illustrate:

✟ **Genesis 2:2-3:**

"And on the seventh day God ended his work which he had made; and he rested on the seventh day from all his work which he had made. And God blessed the seventh day, and sanctified it: because that in it he had rested from all his work which God created and made."

✟ **Exodus 20:11:**

"For [in] six days the LORD made heaven and earth, the sea, and all that in them [is], and rested the seventh day: wherefore the LORD blessed the Sabbath day, and hallowed it."

✟ **Exodus 31:17:**

"It [is] a sign between me and the children of Israel for ever: for [in] six days the LORD made heaven and earth, and on the seventh day he rested, and was refreshed."

✟ **Exodus 35:2:**

"Six days shall work be done, but on the seventh day there shall be to you an holy day, a Sabbath of rest to the

LORD: whosever doeth work therein shall be put to death."

We are now living in the seventh millennium since God created man in His own image, according to Genesis 1:26. The very human body that God, the Creator, made "in His image" from the dust of the earth is made up of 70 percent water. The earth itself also is made up of 70 percent water. We have seven openings, seven holes in our head: two for eyes, two for ears, two for nostrils, and one for a mouth. In addition, there are literally seven parts of the human body: the head, the chest, the loins, two arms, and two legs. There are also seven bones in the neck: the cervical vertebrae. Every seven years, the human body replaces the equivalent of an entirely new skeletal structure.

Seven sets of seven years led the early Jews into the fiftieth year, the year of Jubilee, the year to set the captives free from their debts and enslavement.

There are seven days in every single week that God has given us all.

There are seven continents of the earth:

1. North America
2. South America
3. Africa
4. Europe
5. Asia
6. Australia
7. Antarctica

The fact, that there are seven continents on God's good earth, as well as seven oceans, all presided over by the sevenfold Spirit of God, points to God's ultimate purpose and plan as recorded in Habakkuk 2:14: *"For the earth shall be filled with the knowledge of the glory of the LORD, as the waters cover the sea."*

The Tabernacle of Moses in the Old Testament had seven main aspects in the pattern of worship:

1. The brazen altar for sacrifices.
2. The laver of brass for the priests to wash their hands and feet.
3. The candlestick of pure gold with seven oil lamps for natural light.

4. The table of showbread with twelve loaves of bread – a type of communion.

5. The altar of incense representing a type of prayer.

6. The veil separating the Holy Place from the Holy of Holies (The Most Holy Place).

7. The Ark of the Covenant with the Mercy Seat upon it, which had supernatural light only in the Holy of Holies.

There were also seven main features of the High Priest garments:

1. The mitre

2. Onyx stones on each shoulder of the high priest

3. The breastplate with twelve stones for the twelve tribes of Israel

4. The sash

5. The ephod

6. The robe

7. The tunic made of fine linen

A Kairos Moment – A Crucial Time to Clean Up Our Mess

July 7, 2007, (7-7-7), was the only day in all of human history when all of humanity witnessed the 7th day of the 7th month of the 7th year of the 7th millennium, a major mile marker in human history. It was a significant day that we never saw before and will never see again. That day has come and gone, but it was a major mile marker of a lifetime. Yet far more importantly, this 7th millennium is a time of greater significance that utters and issues forth a clarion call to true repentance from the mouths of the true prophets of God—past, present, and those still to come. This is literally a time to get our own house in order. This is a *kairos* moment.

Kairos is an awesome ancient Greek word that means "God's time" and the "right or opportune moment." The ancient Greeks wisely utilized two distinct words for time: *chronos,* and *kairos*. *Chronos* refers only to the mere ordinary concept of chronological or sequential time, but *kairos* literally points to the extraordinary—a "time in between," one moment in time, a God-given destiny moment, which makes all the difference. In the Greek New Testament, *kairos* is used to refer to "the appointed time in the purpose of God." In this extremely important scriptural sense and context, *kairos* is the time, the destiny moment, when God acts.

Seven Dimensions of Ministry

This is a *kairos* moment, a crucial time to clean up our mess; a *kairos* season, a crucial time to get our business straight. There is no more time to play church. We must occupy until Jesus comes; *not* waste time until Jesus comes, but *occupy* until Jesus Christ comes. We, the local church, must do business in seven detailed dimensions of ministry to positively impact real, life and modern day culture:

1. Spiritually
2. Socially
3. Economically
4. Politically
5. Artistically
6. Culturally
7. Generationally

We must live a life that is totally "rapture-ready," and yet be professionally ready to take care of the necessary business that Christ entrusted us with until that time comes. Yet, the relevant revelation of *seven levels of promise for the overcomer* is not limited to a certain day, month, year, decade, or even millennium.

Seven Main Points of the Model Prayer (The Lord's Prayer)

The classic Model Prayer, better known as the Lord's Prayer, that Jesus taught His very own disciples in Matthew 6:9-13, has a seven-main-point outline for the overcomer.

1. God is the Ultimate Father – *"Our Father which art in heaven,"*
2. The Name of God is Holy – *"Hallowed be thy name."*
3. God is the Ultimate Kingdom Ruler – *"Thy kingdom come,"*
4. God is the Ultimate Authority – *"Thy will be done in earth, as it is in heaven."*
5. God is the Ultimate Source of Provision – *"Give us this day our daily bread."*

6. God Teaches the Ultimate "F"-Word (Forgive) – *"And forgive us our debts, as we forgive our debtors."*

7. God is the Ultimate Deliver – *"And lead us not into temptation, but deliver us from evil: For thine is the kingdom, and the power, and the glory, forever. Amen."*

The relevant revelation of *seven levels of promise for the overcomer* is an eternal truth that powerfully affects our daily public and private prayer and praise experiences. In Psalm 119:164, the writer boldly declares that, *"Seven times a day do I praise thee because of thy righteous judgments."*

The revelation is relevant for your life right now, your death later on, and your life after death, or even the rapture, the great catching away of the church. Are you ready to be a progressive, positive, and powerful rough rider for Jesus Christ right now in your own house, on your own street, and in your own community? Are you ready to let the Revelation be relevant in your life today? Will you let the Revelation be relevant enough in your life to heal your past problems, help your present predicaments, and prepare your God-given purpose for a great

38

future full of divine fulfillment, even in the worst lock-downs of life, the hardcore "Isle of Patmos" imprisonment experiences of life?

The Seven Point Structured Letters for The Seven Churches

In Revelation 1:11, the risen Christ says to John, *"I am Alpha and Omega, the first and the last: and, What thou seest, write in a book, and send it unto the seven churches which are in Asia; unto Ephesus, and unto Smyrna, and unto Pergamos, and unto Thyatira, and unto Sardis, and unto Philadelphia, and unto Laodicea."*

Each of these seven churches in seven different cities in the Roman province of Asia Minor each received a seven-point letter divinely dictated by the Ultimate Overcomer, Jesus Christ Himself. The order in which the churches are listed reflects the very order in which the actual letters were delivered to the actual pastors of those churches.

First of all, each seven-point structured church letter included a consistent greeting with the wording, *"unto the angel of the church,"* figurative language for the pastors of each of these early Christian congregations:

1. Ephesus

2. Smyrna

3. Pergamos

4. Thyatira

5. Sardis

6. Philadelphia

7. Laodicea

Jesus Christ, Himself, divinely dictated the seven letters. Therefore, the very past, present, and future nature of Jesus Christ makes the Revelation relevant for the past, present, and future members of all humanity who will call on Jesus' mighty name. In other words, the timeless classic Book of Revelation speaks directly to us today. In addition, the Book of Revelation influenced the widespread modern-day practice of calling the pastor of a church the "angel of the house," because many persecuted churches under Roman occupation in the earliest years of Christianity actually met in houses. This is a vividly clear reference to Revelation chapters 2 and 3, a concept presented by the Ultimate Pastor, the Shepherd of our souls, Jesus Christ Himself.

Second, each letter to the seven churches of Asia Minor includes a detailed description of the Lord and Savior, Jesus Christ:

1. To the angel of the church of Ephesus, Jesus describes Himself as: *"He that holdeth the seven stars in his right hand, who walketh in the midst of the seven golden candlesticks."*

2. To the angel of the church of Smyrna, Jesus describes Himself as: *"the first and the last, which was dead, and is alive."*

3. To the angel of the church of Pergamos, Jesus describes Himself as: *"He which hath the sharp sword with two edges."*

4. To the angel of the church in Thyatira, Jesus describes Himself as: *"the Son of God, who hath His eyes like unto a flame of fire, and his feet are like fine brass."*

5. To the angel of the church in Sardis, Jesus describes Himself as: *"He that hath the seven Spirits of God, and the seven stars"*.

6. To the angel of the church in Philadelphia, Jesus describes Himself as: *"He that is holy, He that is true, He that hath the key of David, He that openeth, and no man shutteth; and shutteth, and no man openeth."*

7. To the angel of the church of the Laodiceans, Jesus describes Himself as: *"the Amen, the faithful and true witness, the beginning of the creation of God."*

Third, each letter to the seven churches (except for Laodicea) includes a word of commendation from Jesus Christ. All seven churches received the word from Jesus, "I know thy works." Only Laodicea, whose works were neither cold nor hot, but rather lukewarm, was not commended as a church. Therefore, Jesus spat them out of His mouth, and today the majority of Laodicea is buried underground, with the exception of a few ancient ruins that are still visible.

Fourth, Christ gives a bold, straightforward, rebuking, chastening word of condemnation to each church (except Smyrna, the "Martyr Church," and Philadelphia, the "Missionary Church").

Fifth, Christ operates as the ultimate Chief Church Counselor as He gives words of sound eternal truth, wisdom, and divine counsel to each of the seven churches.

Sixth, Christ calls each church to hear, if they have spiritual ears to hear, what the Spirit is saying to that particular congregation.

The seventh structured point in these seven letters to the seven churches is that Jesus Christ, The Ultimate Overcomer, challenges each church to overcome the difficulties and hardships they face, and promises to reward those who do overcome.

We will discuss the importance and relevancy of these seven churches in more detail in chapter two.

Notes For The Overcomer

CHAPTER TWO

The Apostle John — The Author of the Book of Revelation

T he Book of Revelation was written by the apostle John, one of the original 12 disciples of Jesus Christ. John was the disciple who stood at the very foot of the cross when Jesus was crucified. He and his brother, James, were the sons of Zebedee, and together were known as the "sons of thunder." Originally, the two brothers were fishermen, like their father, Zebedee, with whom they trolled their nets in the Lake of Genesareth. Jesus Christ broadened their mission and made them effective fishers of men. John was at first a disciple of John the Baptist, who was a cousin of Jesus. Later, he and James both were numbered, not only among the twelve disciples of Christ, but also, along with Peter, formed the "inner circle" of Jesus' three closest friends and companions.

Seven Key Points about John in the Gospels

1. Peter, James, and John, Jesus' inner circle, were the only three witnesses of the raising of Jairus' daughter (Mark 5:37).

2. Peter, James, and John witnessed the sudden appearing of the prophet Elijah and Lawgiver Moses in an actual meeting with Jesus Christ on the Mount of Transfiguration (Matthew 17:1).

3. Peter, James, and John traveled with Jesus farther into the Garden of Gethsemane, the place of pain and utter agony for Christ, than did the other disciples (Matthew 26:37).

4. John and Peter were sent into the city to prepare for the final Passover meal, better known today as the Last Supper (Luke 22:8).

5. At the Last Supper, which was a Passover *seder* itself, John's place was right next to Jesus Christ, on whose chest he leaned (John 13:23, 25).

6. According to the general interpretation, John was also that "other disciple" who, along with Peter, followed

Jesus after His arrest into the palace of the high priest (John 18:15).

7. John, the "faithful disciple," alone remained near Jesus, at the foot of the cross, with Mary, Jesus' beloved mother, and the other women. At Jesus' direction from the cross, John took Mary into his care (John 19:25-27).

Seven Additional Facts about John

1. After the resurrection of Christ, John and Peter were the first of the disciples to run to the empty tomb.

2. John was the first apostle to believe that Jesus had truly risen from the grave (John 20:2-10).

3. John was accustomed to indicate himself in writing without giving his name, as, *"the disciple whom Jesus loved."*

4. After Jesus' Ascension and the descent of the Holy Spirit, John took, together with Peter, a prominent part in the founding and guidance of the early church.

5. The apostle John was with Peter at the healing of the lame man in the Temple (Acts 3:1).

6. John and Peter both were thrown into prison (Acts 4:3).

7. John and Peter both visited the newly converted Gentiles in Samaria (Acts 8:14).

All of this important history occurred to prepare the beloved apostle John to receive the relevant Revelation of Jesus Christ.

Apparently, the apostle John, in common with the other 11 apostles, remained some 12 years in this first field of labor, Jerusalem, until the persecution of Herod Agrippa I led to the scattering of the apostles from Jerusalem throughout the various provinces of the Roman Empire (Acts 12:1-17). In any case, a messianic community was already in existence at Ephesus before the apostle Paul's first labors there (Acts 18:27). It is easy to connect a sojourn of John in these provinces with the fact that the Holy Spirit did not permit Paul on his second missionary journey to proclaim the gospel in Asia, Mysia and Bithynia (Acts 16:6). Such a sojourn by John in Asia in this first period was neither long nor uninterrupted. He returned with the other disciples to Jerusalem for the Apostolic Council (about A.D. 51). Paul, in opposing his enemies in Galatia, names John explicitly, along with Peter and James "the Just," as a "pillar of the Church". He also refers to the recognition that his apostolic preaching of a gospel free from the law received from these three, the most prominent men of the messianic community at Jerusalem (Galatians 2:9).

In the entire New Testament writings, it is only from the three letters of John and the Book of Revelation that we learn anything further about the apostle John. His letters and the Revelation all presuppose that John belonged to the multitude of personal eyewitnesses of the life and work of Jesus Christ (especially 1 John 1:1-5; 4:14), that he had lived for a long time in Asia Minor, was thoroughly acquainted with the conditions existing in the various messianic communities there, and that he had a position of authority recognized by all messianic communities as leader of this part of the church, even knowing that he was on lock down on the Isle of Patmos. Moreover, the Book of Revelation says that its author, John, was on the island of Patmos when he received the heavenly vision contained in Revelation:

✝ Revelation 1:9:

"I John, who also am your brother, and companion in tribulation, and in the kingdom and patience of Jesus Christ, was in the isle that is called Patmos, for the word of God, and for the testimony of Jesus Christ."

The Relevant Revelation Revealed

A recent article in *Newsweek* magazine entitled, "Religion: Revelation Revealed - Beyond Fear: The Bible's last book is both terrifying and beautiful. But it ends with a message of hope," stated:

John was a passionate, furious Christian, and he had a very clear message, one that resonates strongly with evangelical Christians today: Do not be seduced by the temptations of secular culture. Remain true to Jesus, and God will reward you with heaven. Stray from the path, and the stinking pit awaits. When John wrote his vision, emperor worship had become commonplace throughout the Roman Empire. For Christians this presented an enormous dilemma. On state-sanctioned holidays, the residents of towns ruled by Romans had to make a sacrifice to the emperor-god—for Christians, a violation of the First Commandment.[6]

The Roman authorities sent the apostle John to the Greek island of Patmos, where he wrote the Book of Revelation on lock down. We also know this historically according to the great early church father, Tertullian, who wrote that John was imprisoned on Patmos after being plunged into a boiling pot of oil in Rome, yet emerged unscathed. All of the other apostles had already suffered brutal deaths as early Christian martyrs. Like the great Civil Rights leaders and icons, Rev. Dr. Martin Luther King, Jr., Medger Evers, and young Emmett Till, the original apostles brutally died as martyrs with a Christ-centered mission that made the movement more intense and deeply meaningful.

How The Early Apostles Died – The Blood of The Martyrs

The apostle Peter, who boldly preached the first Christian sermon on the Feast of Pentecost, 50 days after the literal resurrection of Christ, was crucified upside-down because he

---

[6] Lisa Miller, "Religion: Revelation Revealed - Beyond Fear: The Bible's last book is both terrifying and beautiful. But it ends with a message of hope." *Newsweek*, May 24, 2007

did not count himself worthy to die right-side up as had his Lord Jesus Christ. Peter's death as a brave Christian martyr, nailed to an x-shaped cross in Rome, fulfilled Jesus' prophecy recorded in John's Gospel:

❖ **John 21:18-19:**

> *"Verily, verily, I say unto thee, When thou wast young, thou girdest thyself, and walkedst whither thou wouldest: but when thou shalt be old, thou shalt stretch forth thy hands, and another shall gird thee, and carry thee whither thou wouldest not. This spake he, signifying by what death he should glorify God. And when he had spoken this, he saith unto him, Follow me."*

Matthew the apostle suffered martyrdom in Ethiopia, where he was stabbed to death with a sword. As mentioned earlier, the apostle John came face to face with martyrdom when he was boiled in a large pot of oil during a tidal wave of brutal persecution of the Christians in Rome. After supernaturally surviving that death attempt, John was exiled to the dark, dangerous, dismal, and dusty mines on the prison isle of Patmos, where he received the visions from the Lord which, when written down, became known as the Book of Revelation.

John survived his term of imprisonment, and on his release returned to the province of Asia Minor (modern-day Turkey). According to strong tradition, he died an old man in Ephesus, the only apostle (with the possible exception of James, son of Alphaeus, whose fate is unknown) to die peacefully of natural causes.

Although not one of the original twelve apostles, James, the brother of Jesus, the highly esteemed leader of the church in Jerusalem, was literally thrown over one hundred feet down from the southeastern pinnacle of the Temple when he refused to recant his deep abiding faith in his Lord and Savior Jesus Christ. When his tormentors found out that he had survived the fall, they brutally beat him to death with a club. This was the very same pinnacle where Satan took Jesus during His wilderness temptation (see Luke 4:9). James died a courageous Christian martyr.

The apostle Bartholomew, also known as Nathanael, was a well-known missionary to the continent of Asia. Bartholomew boldly witnessed to and advanced the kingdom of God in what is now present-day Turkey, and was martyred for his anointed and powerful Gospel preaching in Armenia, where he was literally whipped to death. Bartholomew died as a courageous Christian martyr.

Like his brother Peter, Andrew the apostle was crucified on an x-shaped cross, but in Greece rather than in Rome. Seven soldiers brutally whipped Andrew before tying him to the x-shaped cross with very strong cords to prolong his intense agony and utterly grueling pain. Christian witnesses to his execution reported that when Andrew was being led to the cross, already in overwhelmingly intense agony, suffering, and pain, spoke these words: "I have long desired and expected this happy hour. The cross has been consecrated by the body of Christ hanging on it." Other reports indicate that Andrew continued to preach the gospel of Jesus Christ to his cruel tormentors for two days, up until the moment he took his very last breath. Andrew died as a courageous Christian martyr.

The apostle Thomas was viciously stabbed to death with a spear in India during one of his faithful missionary journeys to start a Christian church in that particular region of the world. Known for many centuries as "Doubting Thomas," this faithful apostle actually died as an overcomer of the spirit of doubt. Thomas died as a Christian martyr.

Matthias, although not one of the original Twelve, was chosen as an apostle to replace the traitor Judas Iscariot, who hanged himself. He qualified as an apostle because of his faithfulness from the time Jesus was baptized by John the Baptist until He ascended on high before 500 witnesses. And, like most of his colleagues, Matthias did not die a natural death, but was brutally stoned and then beheaded for the cause of Christ. Matthias died as a Christian martyr.

Paul, also known as Saul was commissioned as an apostle by the risen Christ himself, after an early career as persecutor of the church. In a ministry spanning thirty years or more, Paul was a highly effective preacher, teacher, missionary, and writer of the gospel of Christ. By order of the evil Roman Emperor Nero, Paul was tortured and beheaded in A.D. 67 in Rome. Paul died as a Christian martyr.

Such harsh persecution and martyrdom was the daily backdrop of life in the early church for many years. This was the general environment, setting, and atmosphere in which John, the beloved apostle received the vivid visions that formed the basis the last book of the Bible, the Book of Revelation.

These apostles of the early church did not just merely talk about the Kingdom of God, they put their very lives on the line to advance it every day in every way they could. Lisa Miller goes on to state in her *Newsweek* article that, "Revelation was written as a letter to the Christians of Asia Minor and was probably read aloud wherever they gathered. For John's audience, the book would have been a dramatic step beyond the Jewish apocalypses that preceded it, like watching a Technicolor movie after a lifetime of black and white."[7]

The Four Vivid "In the Spirit" Visions of Revelation

The Book of Revelation is structured around four distinct and vivid visions that John received, which were all outlined in various details of sevens. Each of the four visions begins with the classic words *"in the Spirit"*. These four visions take the reader from John's imprisonment on the Isle of Patmos, to the throne in Heaven, into the wilderness, and, finally, to the New Jerusalem.

---

[7] Ibid; Miller, *Newsweek*

✝ **Revelation 1:10:**

"I was in the Spirit on the Lord's Day, and heard behind me a great voice, as of a trumpet."

✝ **Revelation 4:2:**

"And immediately I was in the spirit: and, behold, a throne was set in heaven, and one sat on the throne."

✝ **Revelation 17:3:**

*"So he carried me away **in the spirit** into the wilderness: and I saw a woman sit upon a scarlet colored beast, full of names of blasphemy, having seven heads and ten horns."*

✝ **Revelation 21:10:**

*"And he carried me away **in the spirit** to a great and high mountain, and shewed me that great city, the holy Jerusalem, descending out of heaven from God."*

The Book of Revelation literally takes the reader from a world of harsh imprisonment to a new Heaven and a new earth. No wonder we are promised a blessing for reading, hearing, and keeping the sayings found in the book.

Early Church Fathers Confirm the Apostle John as Author of the Book of Revelation

In his later years, the apostle John mentored Polycarp, who went on to become the revered and highly respected Bishop of Smyrna, the suffering church, one of the seven churches of Asia Minor actually mentioned in the Book of Revelation. This was an important link, because Polycarp was able to carry on John's visions and message of the Ultimate Overcomer, Jesus Christ, to another age and another level. According to the early church father, Irenaeus, Polycarp attributed the writing of the Book of Revelation to his old mentor, the apostle John, near the end of the reign of Roman Emperor Domitian (AD 81-96).

Domitian demanded that all his subjects declare him as "Lord and God." Most mature Christians of that day would rather die as martyrs (and many did) rather than compromise their blood-bought Christian faith by calling Domitian "Lord and God". Ever since Nero's reign of horror in the mid 60s (during which time both Peter and Paul were martyred), the early Christian believers had been discriminated against and were called the enemies of all humanity due to their daily practice of "illegal" religious activities. This historical information sheds light on the meaning of the Book of Revelation as originally addressed to the generations of severely persecuted Christians alive at the time of its writing. Like the classic old Negro Spirituals, many of which were inspired directly by the visions and content of the Book of Revelation, the Revelation itself contains many symbols that can only be understood by studying the high-tension discriminatory climate against Christians in the first century, the clashing of cultures in crisis, the social-economic background, and history of the people in the text. Yet even more importantly, the historic scriptural text itself unveils and uncovers itself when studied in the proper context.

In her *Newsweek* article, Miller goes on to state concerning the modern day relevancy of the book of Revelation on today's society:

John's dream became the Book of Revelation, the final book of the Christian Bible, a vision of heaven and the end of the world that is probably the most scrutinized yet inscrutable piece of literature in history. Heaven's pearly gates and gold-paved streets, found everywhere from Negro spirituals to New Yorker cartoons, have their roots in Revelation. The work, which has formed the West's understanding of the afterlife, must be read with care. Passages taken out of historical or literary context can make Christianity appear violent and vengeful, when the book is in fact rich in images of mercy and, like the Old Testament prophet Isaiah, holds out the promise of ultimate order and forgiveness."[8]

Jesus Christ Himself, is the one Who gives the revelation to John. Therefore, the book really is the Revelation of Jesus Christ to the church, past, present, and future. Here is the key verse in the Book of Revelation that unlocks its relevant eternal truth for all times:

✟ **Revelation 1:19:**

"Write the things which thou hast seen, and the things which are, and the things which shall be hereafter."

Unveil—Pull the Covers Off

The Book of Revelation unveils, uncovers, reveals, and explains itself. Chapter 1 represents *"the things which thou hast*

---

[8] Ibid, Miller, Newsweek

seen." Chapters two and three represent *"the things which are."* Chapters four through twenty-two represent *"the things which shall be hereafter."* This one verse describes the whole book in a nutshell. So let's crack it open, read further, and let it unveil its true meaning.

1. The things you have seen: the relevant past.
2. The things, which are: the relevant present—relevant right now.
3. The things hereafter: the relevant future.

The Book of Revelation also holds the great distinction of being the only prophetic book found in the entire New Testament, as compared to the 17 prophetic books, both the major and minor categories combined, in the Old Testament.

The Book of Revelation says that there is a threefold blessing for actually reading it, because it means to reveal, not to cover up. The Greek word for revelation is *apokalupsis* (pronounced *ah pah-kah-loop-sis*), which means disclosure; appearing, coming, lighten, manifestation, be revealed. The word revelation also means to unveil, making known what was previously hidden, and to pull the covers off. It is time to pull the covers off of ignorance, reposition ourselves, and realize that the revelation is relevant for everyday living. Bishop T. D.

Jakes writes, "In Scripture, revelation often literally means to 'unveil'. The most powerful relationships we can have are with those who help us to see what we didn't see before. A church or school or even a friend who unveils possibilities and potential becomes a limitless resource to those of us who are upwardly mobile".[9]

A Benefit to the Believer

The Book of Revelation is a benefit to the present day believer. It is a benefit to the community. Moreover, it is a benefit to the members of modern day society to read this entire prophetic book. In a summary of the Book of Revelation, entitled: *Revelation – The Revealing of Jesus to the World*, Dr. John C. Maxwell states: "The Book of Revelation differs from every other New Testament book. It contains not only a message for the first century church, to whom it was written, but also to the church through the ages, particularly those living in the 'end times' who will see Christ return to earth." [10]

---

[9] T. D. Jakes, *Reposition Yourself – Living Life Without Limits*. (New York: Atria Books, 2007), pg 47

[10] John C. Maxwell, "Revelation—The Revealing of Jesus to the World," *The Maxwell Leadership Bible*. (Nashville: Thomas Nelson Publishers, 2002), pg 1557

Revelation 1:3 brings out this important three fold blessing of reading the book when it says: *"Blessed is he that readeth, and they that hear the words of this prophecy, and keep those things which are written therein: for the time is at hand."* We must realize that the time is at hand, so therefore we must: 1.) Read the Revelation. 2.) Hear the Revelation. 3.) Keep the sayings of the Revelation. The time is at hand, and the revelation is relevant for today.

Dr. Benjamin Mays

Dr. Benjamin E. Mays, educator, author, distinguished theologian, former president of Morehouse College, and respected civil rights activist, was right on target with his classic little poem, "God's Minute":

> I've only just a minute,
> Only sixty seconds in it.
> Forced upon me, can't refuse it,
> Didn't seek it, didn't choose it,
> But it's up to me to use it.
> I must suffer if I lose it,
> Give an account if I abuse it,
> Just a tiny little minute,

But eternity is in it.[11]

---

[11] Dr. Benjamin Mays, God's Minute, the world renown educator's classic poem

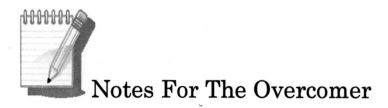

Notes For The Overcomer

CHAPTER THREE

The Basic Seven Main Point Outline of the Book of Revelation

There a seven main points that we can take from the Book of Revelation. They are as follows:

1. Seven Churches of Asia Minor (Rev. 1:9-3:22)

2. Seven Seals (Rev. 4:1-8:1)

3. Seven Trumpets (Rev. 8:2-11:8)

4. Seven Significant Signs (Rev. 11:9-15:4)

5. Seven Vials (Rev.15:5-16:21)

6. Seven Significant Scenes (Rev. 17:1-20:3)

7. Seven Vivid Views of Consummation (Rev. 20:4-22:5)

This is not merely a coincidence. The consistency of the seven-point outline in the writings of the apostle John is living proof that the entire Book of Revelation was divinely inspired by God to be the last book of the Bible, and the only book of prophecy in the entire New Testament. The number seven, the number of completion, rest, and, most of all, significance, is mentioned fifty-two times in the Book of Revelation. These fifty-two references indicate clearly the prominence not only of the number seven in the Book of Revelation, but also the importance of numerical symbolism as a whole. In the Book of Revelation, as throughout the entire Bible, numbers often embody symbolic as well as literal meanings. Therefore, the symbolic references provide greater levels and more in-depth dimensions of meaning to the literal connotations, such as the symbolic seven candlesticks and seven stars, and the literal seven persecuted churches of Asia Minor, along with their actual individual pastors, and the literal Seven-fold Spirit of God.

The numbers most commonly used in Scripture, along with their powerful symbolic values, are:

1—Unity, One God, Monotheism, primacy, independent existence (Deuteronomy 6:4).

2—Agreement, an addition; hence, strength, help, confirmation (Ecclesiastes 4:9–12).

3—Trinity, Father, Son and Holy Spirit; Faith, Hope, and Love; The simplest compound unity; the number for God (Matthew 28:19).

4—The world with its four seasons and directions (Revelation 7:1).

5—The number associated with grace, Man, as portrayed by the various five-membered parts of the body (Leviticus 14:14–16).

6—Consummate evil, failure (Revelation 13:18), because it falls short of perfection, which is represented by the number seven.

7—The number of rest, completion, perfection, and significance. A number representing earth crowned with heaven, the latter lending perfection or completeness to the former (Revelation 1:4).

10—Five doubled; hence human completeness (Revelation 2:10).

12.—The number of God's government. Twelve Tribes of Israel. Twelve apostles. Twelve Gates in the New Jerusalem.

God's perfect manifestation of Himself to the created order (Revelation 21:12).

Now let us look closely at a more detailed outline of the Book of Revelation. It is extremely important to be totally aware of the good, the bad, and the indifferent aspects unveiled in the Book of Revelation in order to obtain the thoroughly life-changing motivation that it promises. You cannot truly appreciate any of the seven blessings of the Book of Revelation without understanding the highly intense, jagged-edged, hard-core judgments detailed there. It is important to read the whole Book of Revelation. The tradition nowadays is to overlook the harsh details of the Book of Revelation, but there is no way to become a people of substance without getting the whole message as intended by God Himself.

Detailed Outline of the Book of Revelation

I. **Seven churches of Asia Minor (Revelation 1:9–3:22)** (inspiration for the Civil Rights anthem, "We Shall Overcome")

II. **Seven seals (Revelation 4:1–8:1)**

  A. The setting (Revelation 4:1–5:14)

1. Be at the meeting around the throne (Revelation 4:1–11) (inspiration for the songs "Be At The Meeting," "Two Wings," and "Holy, Holy, Holy")

2. The Lamb opens a book sealed with seven seals. The Lamb is the Lion of the Tribe of Judah (Revelation 5:1–14) (inspiration for the many songs concerning the Lamb)

B. The seven seals **(Revelation 6:1–8:1)**

1. First seal: White Horse - An Anti-Christ crowned conqueror (Revelation 6:1-2)

2. Second seal: Red Horse –War and violent death (Revelation 6:3-4)

3. Third seal: Black Horse – Famine (Revelation 6:5-6)

4. Fourth seal: Pale Horse – Death and hell (massive death of ¼ of all humanity alive during the Tribulation) (Revelation 6:7-8)

5. Fifth seal: The souls of the slain under the altar (Revelation 6:9–11)

6. Sixth seal: The Great Day of His wrath (Revelation 6:12–17) (inspiration for the old Negro Spiritual "Great

Day," featuring classic wording taken from Revelation 6:7: *"who shall be able to stand?")*

a. First Interlude: 144,000 sealed (Revelation 7:1–8)

b. Second Interlude: A great multitude (Revelation 7:9–17) (inspiration for the many "These Are They" songs)

7. Seventh seal: Silence in Heaven (Revelation 8:1)

The classic Old Negro Spiritual entitled "Going To Heaven", which is an awesome musical work done by enslaved Africans who did not even read or write English at that time speaks directly to the subject matter of "The Book of Revelation", "The Book of Seven Seals" and "that bleeding Lamb" in the first verse of the historic song. The oppressed and enslaved Africans in America and their descendents literally memorized scripture preached in southern revival meetings and wrote meaningful lyrics and music that would change the whole world forever.

Going to Heaven

The Book of Revelation God to us revealed

Mysteries of salvation, **The Book of Seven Seals**.

Going to heaven,

Going to heaven,

Going to heaven to see **that bleeding Lamb.**[12]

III. Seven trumpets (Revelation 8:2–11:18)

A. The setting: The golden altar (Revelation 8:2–6)

B. The seven trumpets (Revelation 8:7–11:18)

1. First trumpet: Hail and fire mingled with blood on the earth – 1/3 of all the trees and grass destroyed during the Tribulation (Revelation 8:7)

2. Second trumpet: 1/3 of the sea turns into blood; 1/3 of the fish of the sea die; and 1/3 of all ships destroyed (Revelation 8:8-9)

3. Third trumpet: 1/3 of the rivers become Wormwood; many men die due to the bitter waters (Revelation 8:10-11)

4. Fourth trumpet: Sun, moon, and stars darkened; 1/3 of the day is darkened; 1/3 of the night is extended (Revelation 8:12)

---

12 Going To Heaven, Old Negro Spiritual

5. Fifth trumpet: First woe—The bottomless pit and demonic locusts that will torment mankind for five months during the Tribulation (Revelation 8:3–9:12)

6. Sixth trumpet: Second woe—cavalry; Four angels loosed; Horses with heads of lions which kill 1/3 of men with fire, smoke, and brimstone out of their mouths (Revelation 9:13–21)

    a. First interlude: The apostle John eats the little book (Revelation 10:1–11)

    b. Second interlude: Two witnesses (believed to be Moses and Elijah by many Bible scholars) (Revelation 11:1–14)

7. Seventh trumpet: Third woe—voices in Heaven (Revelation 11:15–18)

IV. Seven significant signs (Revelation 11:9–15:4)

A. The setting: the Ark of the Covenant (Revelation 11:19)

B. The seven significant signs (Revelation 12:1–15:4)

1. The woman—Israel; the dragon—Satan; the child—Jesus, the Ultimate Overcomer; the war in Heaven and the war on Earth (Revelation 12:1–17)

2. The beast from the sea (Revelation 13:1–10)

3. The beast from the earth (Revelation 13:11–18)

4. The Lamb and the 144,000 (Revelation 14:1–5) (Revelation 14 is the inspiration for "The Battle Hymn of the Republic")

5. Four proclamations (Revelation 14:6–13)

6. The harvest of the earth is ripe (Revelation 14:14–20)

7. The seven angels and the song of Moses and the song of the Lamb (Revelation 15:1–4) (Points to the importance singing old hymns and new worship songs)

V. The seven vials of God's wrath (Revelation 15:5–16:21)

A. The setting: The tent of witness (Revelation 15:5–16:1)

B. Seven vials of God's wrath (Revelation 16:2–21)

1. First vial of wrath: Earth – Sores on men who have the mark of the beast (Revelation 16:2)

2. Second vial of wrath: Sea – Sea becomes as blood of dead men (Revelation 16:3)

3. Third vial of wrath: Rivers and fountains of water become blood (Revelation 16:4–7)

4. Fourth vial of wrath: Sun – Men scorched with great heat (Revelation 16:8-9)

5. Fifth vial of wrath: The throne of the beast full of darkness and gnawing of tongues in pain (Revelation 16:10-11)

6. Sixth vial of wrath: Euphrates River is dried up (Revelation 16:12)

a. Interlude: three unclean spirits (Revelation 16:13–16)

7. Seventh vial of wrath: the cities of the nations (Revelation 16:17–21)

VI. Seven significant scenes (Revelation 17:1–20:3)

A. The setting: A wilderness (Revelation 17:1–3)

B. The significant scenes (Revelation 17:3–20:3)

1. Scene 1- A woman on a scarlet beast (Revelation 17:3–5)

2. Scene 2 - The mystery of the woman and the beast (Revelation 17:6–18)

3. Scene 3 - Seven voices: Babylon fallen (Revelation 18:1–19:10)

4. Scene 4 - King of kings and Lord of lords (Revelation 19:11–16) (inspiration for the "Hallelujah Chorus")

5. Scene 5 - The supper of the great God (Revelation 19:17-18)

6. Scene 6 - The war (Revelation 19:19–21)

7. Scene 7 - Satan bound for a thousand years (Revelation 20:1–3)

VII. The vivid views of the consummation (Revelation 20:4–22:5)

A. The setting (Revelation 20:4–10)

1. Living and reigning with Christ (Revelation 20:4–6)

2. Satan released to deceive (Revelation 20:7–10)

B. The scenes (Revelation 20:1–22:5)

1. Vivid view 1- The great white throne (Revelation 20:11)

2. Vivid view 2 -The last judgment (Revelation 20:12–15)

3. Vivid view 3 -The new heaven and new earth (Revelation 21:1)

4. Vivid view 4 -The New Jerusalem (Revelation 21:2–8) (Inspiration for the old Negro Spiritual "Walk in Jerusalem Just Like John")

5. Vivid view 5 - The bride of the Lamb (Revelation 21:9–21)

6. Vivid view 6 - The light of God's presence (Revelation 21:22–27)

7. Vivid view 7 - Paradise regained (Revelation 22:1–5)

VIII. Epilogue (Revelation 22:6–21)

A. Seven confirming witnesses (Revelation 22:6–17)

B. Final warning and assurance (Revelation 22:18–20)

C. Benediction (Revelation 22:21)

The theme of the relevant revelation of seven is found not only in the Book of Revelation, but also in the Gospel of John, which was also written by John the apostle. Early church fathers: Hippolytus, Origen, Tertullian, and Clement of Alexandria, all testified that the apostle John was the writer of the Gospel and the three epistles that bear his name, as well as the Book of Revelation. In the Gospel of John, Jesus Christ, the Ultimate Overcomer, performs seven profound miracles prior to His resurrection from the dead.

Seven Significant Miracles of Jesus in the Gospel of John Prior to the Resurrection

1. Changing water into wine at the wedding in Cana at Galilee (John 2:1-11).
2. Healing of the nobleman's son (John 4:46-54).
3. Healing of the paralytic man at the pool of Bethesda (John 5:1-39).
4. Feeding of the 5000 (John 6:1-14), the only miracle reported in all four Gospels: (see also Matthew 14:13-21; Mark 6:32-34; Luke 9:10-17).
5. Walking on the water (John 6:15-21, see also Matthew 14:22-36; Mark 6:45-56).
6. Healing of the man blind from birth at the pool of Siloam (John 9:1-41).
7. Raising of Lazarus from the dead (John 11:1-44).

The Gospel of John also has seven distinct witnesses who boldly declare that Jesus is the Son of God.

The Seven Witnesses Declaring that Jesus Is the Son of God

John's stated purpose for writing his Gospel was that those who read it would know that Jesus Christ was the Son of God and the Savior of the world:

✝ **John 20:31:**

"These are written, that ye might believe that Jesus is the Christ, the Son of God, and that believing ye might have life through his name."

John brings seven witnesses to the stand to testify to this eternal truth:

1. John the Baptist: *"This is the Son of God"* (John 1:34).
2. Nathanael: *"Thou art the Son of God"* (John 1:49).
3. Peter: *"Thou art that Christ, the Son of the living God"* (John 6:69).
4. Martha: *"Thou art the Christ, the Son of God"* (John 11:27).
5. Thomas (to Jesus): *"My Lord and my God"* (John 20:28).
6. John himself: *"Jesus is the Christ, the Son of God"* (John 20:31).

7. Christ Himself: *"I...am he"* (the Messiah, to the Samaritan woman at the well), (John 4:26); *"I and my Father are one"* (John 10:30); *"I am the Son of God"* (John 10:36), *"He that hath seen me hath seen the Father"* (John 14:9).

Another unique feature of the Gospel of John is that it contains the classic seven "I Am" statements of Jesus.

The Seven "I Am" Statements of Jesus Christ

1. *"I am the bread of life"* (John 6:35)
2. *"I am the light of the world"* (John 8:12)
3. *"I am the door"* (John 10:7, 9)
4. *"I am the good shepherd"* (John 10:11)
5. *"I am the resurrection and the life"* (John 11:25)
6. *"I am the way, and the truth, and the life"* (John 14:6)
7. *"I am the true vine"* (John 15:1)

The seven miracles, seven witnesses, and seven "I Am" statements found in the Gospel of John all point to the fact that God was preparing John to receive the Lord's revelation, with all of its intense references to seven churches, seven seals, seven trumpets, seven signs, seven vials, seven spectacles, and seven sights of consummation. This is certainly no coincidence—this is eternal truth.

Jesus Christ, the Ultimate Overcomer, even made seven last statements from the cross at Calvary.

Seven Last Sayings of Jesus Christ on the Cross

1. *"Father, forgive them, for they know not what they do"* (Luke 23:34).

2. *"Verily I say unto thee, today shalt thou be with me in paradise"*
   (Luke 23:43).

3. *"Woman, behold thy son"* (to His mother, Mary, John 19:26); *"Behold thy mother"* (to John, the beloved apostle, John 19:27). With these words, Jesus commended his mother, who likely was a widow, into John's care.

4. *"Eloi Eloi lama sabachthani?"* ("My God, My God, why hast thou forsaken me?" Mark 15:34; see also Matthew 27:46)

5. *"I thirst"* (John 19:28).

6. *"It is finished"* (John 19:30).

7. *"Father, into thy hands I commend my spirit"* (Luke 23:46).

Seventy Times Seven: The Power of Forgiveness

It is no coincidence that the revelation of seven, the number of great significance in the Bible, nature, culture, and history, is extremely relevant to the gospel, life, death, and resurrection of Jesus Christ, as well as to the life of His church. The scriptural concept of 70 x 7 is synonymous with Jesus Christ, the Ultimate Overcomer, and is a profound teaching concerning God's eternal forgiveness expressed through our own lives. Matthew 18:21-22 in the New King James version of the Bible declares: *"Then Peter came to Him and said, 'Lord, how often shall my brother sin against me, and I forgive him? Up to seven times?' Jesus said to him, 'I do not say to you, up to seven times, but up to seventy times seven.'"*

Jesus Christ is not telling us here to forgive our brothers or sisters in Christ, our neighbors, or even our enemies, only 490 times, but to forgive them as often as necessary. (Hopefully, by the time you have truly forgiven someone 490 times, you will by then have developed a pattern of true forgiveness.) Please note that forgiveness is not agreement with unjust or evil actions, or consent to the ways of the wrongdoer. Forgiveness is actually the God factor that frees up the victim to become the victor. Forgiveness enables the abused to become overcomers through the blood of the Lamb and the word of their testimony. In these verses Christ is telling us that we must always forgive our brothers and sisters in life when they have sinned against us. God the Father has totally forgiven us all of our horrible sins (as long as we have truly repented), and it would be completely wrong and totally unjust for us to deny forgiveness to others. The power to forgive releases you from the bondage of anger that need not become a stumbling block of deep sin to pull you down into deep depression, hatred, violence, and self-defeating negative behavior patterns.

St. Francis of Assisi

I often think of the classic life changing prayer attributed to St. Francis of Assisi:

> Lord, make me an instrument of your peace;
>
> Where there is hatred, let me sow love;
>
> Where there is injury, pardon;
>
> Where there is doubt, faith;
>
> Where there is despair, hope;
>
> Where there is darkness, light;
>
> Where there is sadness, joy;
>
> O Divine Master,
>
> Grant that I may not so much seek
>
> To be consoled as to console;
>
> To be understood, as to understand;
>
> To be loved, as to love;
>
> For it is in giving that we receive,
>
> It is in pardoning that we are pardoned,

And it is in dying that we are born to eternal life.[13]

The Seven Spirits of God

Four times the Book of Revelation makes mention of the "seven spirits of God" (Rev.1:4; 3:1; 4:5; 5:6). This unusual phrase refers to the workings, the personality, and the dynamics of the Holy Spirit. Isaiah 11:2 gives us a sevenfold description of the Holy Spirit that identifies the seven distinct ways the Spirit moves and expresses Himself:

1. The Spirit of the Lord
2. The Spirit of wisdom
3. The Spirit of understanding
4. The Spirit of counsel
5. The Spirit of might
6. The Spirit of knowledge
7. The Spirit of the fear of the Lord.

---

[13] St. Francis of Assisi concerning being an instrument of peace

The Number Seven In the Book of Revelation

The Book of Revelation refers to the number "seven" or the word "seventh" in 36 verses in 14 of its 22 chapters. This repetitive use of the number seven provides the framework for the entire book. A quick survey of these verses, which are given below, bears this out:

The Seven Churches of Asia Minor

1) Revelation 1:4

*"John to the **seven** churches which are in Asia: Grace be unto you, and peace, from him which is, and which was, and which is to come; and from the **seven** Spirits which are before his throne."*

2) Revelation 1:11

*"Saying, I am Alpha and Omega, the first and the last: and, What thou seest, write in a book, and send it unto the **seven** churches which are in Asia; unto Ephesus, and unto Smyrna, and unto Pergamos, and unto Thyatira, and unto Sardis, and unto Philadelphia, and unto Laodicea."*

Seven Golden Candlesticks

3) Revelation 1:12

*"And I turned to see the voice that spake with me. And being turned, I saw **seven** golden candlesticks."*

4) Revelation 1:13

*"And in the midst of the **seven** candlesticks one like unto the Son of man, clothed with a garment down to the foot, and girt about the paps with a golden girdle."*

The Seven Stars

5) Revelation 1:16

*"And he had in his right hand **seven** stars: and out of his mouth went a sharp two-edged sword: and his countenance was as the sun shineth in his strength."*

The Mystery Revealed

The Seven Stars are the Seven Angels (Pastors) and the Seven Candlesticks are the Seven Churches

6) Revelation 1:20

*"The mystery of the **seven** stars which thou sawest in my right hand, and the **seven** golden candlesticks. The **seven** stars are the angels of the **seven** churches: and the **seven** candlesticks which thou sawest are the **seven** churches."*

7) Revelation 2:1

*"Unto the angel of the church of Ephesus write; These things saith he that holdeth the **seven** stars in his right hand, who walketh in the midst of the **seven** golden candlesticks."*

The Seven Lamps are the Seven Spirits of God

8) Revelation 3:1

*"And unto the angel of the church in Sardis write; These things saith he that hath the **seven** Spirits of God, and the **seven** stars; I know thy works, that thou hast a name that thou livest, and art dead."*

9) Revelation 4:5

*"And out of the throne proceeded lightnings and thunderings and voices: and there were **seven** lamps of fire burning before the throne, which are the **seven** Spirits of God."*

The Seven Seals

10) Revelation 5:1

*"And I saw in the right hand of him that sat on the throne a book written within and on the backside, sealed with **seven** seals."*

11) Revelation 5:5

*"And one of the elders saith unto me, Weep not: behold, the Lion of the tribe of Judah, the Root of David, hath prevailed to open the book, and to loose the **seven** seals thereof."*

The Lamb's Seven Horns and Seven Eyes are the Seven Spirits of God

12) Revelation 5:6

*"And I beheld, and, lo, in the midst of the throne and of the four beasts, and in the midst of the elders, stood a Lamb as it had been slain, having **seven** horns and **seven** eyes, which are the **seven** Spirits of God sent forth into all the earth."*

From the surrounding context it is clear that this Lamb that was slain which has seven horns and seven eyes (the sevenfold Holy Spirit) refers symbolically to Jesus Christ. However, we must acknowledge that the apostle John literally saw a Lamb with seven horns in his vision. Many would say that to claim even to have a vision concerning any such thing is pure nonsense. Nevertheless, in July 2007, a seven-legged lamb was born in New Zealand. If such a creature could be born in our lifetime, just imagine what could happen in the future. What the apostle John saw in the Book of Revelation, both symbolic and literal, used to seem foolish to the public, but time has a way of proving that the revelation is relevant.

The Seventh Seal—Silence in Heaven

13) Revelation 8:1

*"And when he had opened the **seven**th seal, there was silence in heaven about the space of half an hour."*

I have never experienced the half an hour of silence in Heaven, but I have often experienced silence from Heaven down here on earth. I know personally what it is to serve God even when He is extremely silent. Sometimes, when God seems silent as we go through the turbulent storms of life, we have to remember what He has already told us. The silence of God is a key factor in bringing maturity to a Christian's walk with the Lord.

Recently my wife, Brenda, and I, along with our children: Yolanda, Jordan, and Faith, took a much needed vacation to see Brenda's parents and family in Youngstown, Ohio. After crossing both the Throgs Neck and George Washington bridges and getting on I-80 West in route to our desired destination, we drove through a turbulent rainstorm. It rained so hard that I could see only the white lines on the road and the yellow, orange, and red signs along the side of the road. I could not even see the side of the road—only the signs.

Prior to the beginning of the storm, the children were asking every few minutes those classic travel questions: "Are we there yet?" "How many more miles until we get there?" Yet during that turbulent, heavy rainstorm on I-80 West, somewhere high in the Appalachian Mountains of Pennsylvania, there was complete silence in our SUV for the space of about half an hour. Aside from the rain itself, the only sounds that broke that silence were the several times Brenda asked me to pull over to the side of the road.

After half an hour of non-stop heavy rain, the storm ended, the sun came out, and the spirit of silence in the SUV subsided. We made it safely to our destination. Sometimes we all have to experience the silence of God during the turbulent storms of life. Remember, no storm lasts forever. There is always sunshine after the storm.

Seven Angels with Seven Trumpets

14) Revelation 8:2

*"And I saw the **seven** angels which stood before God; and to them were given **seven** trumpets."*

15) Revelation 8:6

*"And the **seven** angels which had the **seven** trumpets prepared themselves to sound."*

Seven Thunders' Utterance Sealed Up

16) Revelation 10:3

*"And cried with a loud voice, as when a lion roareth: and when he had cried, **seven** thunders uttered their voices."*

17) Revelation 10:4

*"And when the **seven** thunders had uttered their voices, I was about to write: and I heard a voice from heaven saying unto me, Seal up those things which the **seven** thunders uttered, and write them not."*

The Seventh Angel—The Mystery of God Should be Finished

18) Revelation 10:7

*"But in the days of the voice of the **seven**th angel, when he shall begin to sound, the mystery of God should be finished, as he hath declared to his servants the prophets."*

Seven Thousand Slain Men

19) Revelation 11:13

*"And the same hour was there a great earthquake, and the tenth part of the city fell, and in the earthquake were slain of men **seven** thousand: and the remnant were affrighted, and gave glory to the God of heaven."*

The Seventh Angel Sounded

20) Revelation 11:15

*"And the **seven**th angel sounded; and there were great voices in heaven, saying, The kingdoms of this world are become the kingdoms of our Lord, and of his Christ; and he shall reign for ever and ever."*

A Great Red Dragon with Seven Heads, Ten Horns, and Seven Crowns

21) Revelation 12:3

"And there appeared another wonder in heaven; and behold a great red dragon, having **seven** *heads and ten horns, and* **seven** *crowns upon his heads."*

22) Revelation 13:1

"And I stood upon the sand of the sea, and saw a beast rise up out of the sea, having **seven** *heads and ten horns, and upon his horns ten crowns, and upon his heads the name of blasphemy."*

The Seven Last Plagues

23) Revelation 15:1

"And I saw another sign in heaven, great and marvelous, **seven** *angels having the* **seven** *last plagues; for in them is filled up the wrath of God."*

24) Revelation 15:6

"And the **seven** *angels came out of the temple, having the* **seven** *plagues, clothed in pure and white linen, and having their breasts girded with golden girdles."*

The Seven Golden Vials

25) Revelation 15:7

*"And one of the four beasts gave unto the **seven** angels **seven** golden vials full of the wrath of God, who liveth forever and ever."*

26) Revelation 15:8

*"And the temple was filled with smoke from the glory of God, and from his power; and no man was able to enter into the temple, till the **seven** plagues of the **seven** angels were fulfilled."*

27) Revelation 16:1

*"And I heard a great voice out of the temple saying to the **seven** angels, Go your ways, and pour out the vials of the wrath of God upon the earth."*

28) Revelation 16:17

*"And the **seven**th angel poured out his vial into the air; and there came a great voice out of the temple of heaven, from the throne, saying, It is done."*

29) Revelation 17:1

*"And there came one of the **seven** angels which had the **seven** vials, and talked with me, saying unto me, Come hither; I will shew unto thee the judgment of the great whore that sitteth upon many waters:"*

The Scarlet Colored Beast with Seven Heads and Ten Horns

30) Revelation 17:3

*"So he carried me away in the spirit into the wilderness: and I saw a woman sit upon a scarlet coloured beast, full of names of blasphemy, having **seven** heads and ten horns."*

31) Revelation 17:7

*"And the angel said unto me, Wherefore didst thou marvel? I will tell thee the mystery of the woman, and of the beast that carrieth her, which hath the **seven** heads and ten horns."*

The Seven Heads are Seven Mountains

32) Revelation 17:9

*"And here is the mind which hath wisdom. The **seven** heads are **seven** mountains, on which the woman sitteth."*

The Seven Kings

33) Revelation 17:10

*"And there are **seven** kings: five are fallen, and one is, and the other is not yet come; and when he cometh, he must continue a short space."*

The Eighth is of the Seven

34) Revelation 17:11

*"And the beast that was, and is not, even he is the eighth, and is of the **seven**, and goeth into perdition."*

The Bride – The Lamb's Wife

35) Revelation 21:9

*"And there came unto me one of the **seven** angels which had the **seven** vials full of the **seven** last plagues, and talked with me, saying, Come hither, I will shew thee the bride, the Lamb's wife."*

The Seventh Stone

36) Revelation 21:20

*"The fifth, sardonyx; the sixth, sardius; the **seventh**, chrysolyte; the eighth, beryl; the ninth, a topaz; the tenth, a chrysoprasus; the eleventh, a jacinth; the twelfth, an amethyst."*

These various scriptures that mention the word seven or seventh help to give a better picture of the subject matter of the Book of Revelation. Richard Bauckham states in his article entitled "Understanding Revelation":

"Revelation's continued relevance to later readers lies in its power to bring this heavenly perspective to bear on every situation in which God's rule appears to be subverted by the powers of the world. Its purpose is not to give mere information about the future, but to enable Christians to live in the way that God's final purpose for the world requires." [14]

---

[14] Richard Bauckham, "Understanding Revelation," *Zondervan Handbook to the Bible*, (Grand Rapids, MI: Zondervan Publishing House) 771.

When we talk about *Seven Levels of Promise for the Overcomer*, we are talking about each of the seven churches addressed in chapters two and three of Revelation, and we need to realize that we are talking about seven historical churches. At the same time, however, we are also talking about seven personality traits alive within the church today. We all need the seven Spirits of God—the sevenfold Holy Spirit—to move mightily in our lives today. We need the help of the Spirit of the Lord, the Spirit of wisdom, the Spirit of understanding, the Spirit of counsel, the Spirit of power, the Spirit of knowledge, and the Spirit of the fear of the Lord in order to deal with each of the temptations that arose within the churches of Ephesus, Smyrna, Pergamos, Thyatira, Sardis, Philadelphia, and Laodicea.

When we allow the Spirit of the Lord, the very first aspect of the seven Spirits of God to move in our situation the enemy will have to flee seven ways. Deuteronomy 28:7: *"The LORD shall cause thine enemies that rise up against thee to be smitten before thy face: they shall come out against thee one way, and flee before thee seven ways."* The Lord shall cause your enemies to rise up against you so the Spirit of the Lord can show up on the scene with the Spirit of wisdom, the Spirit of understanding, the Spirit of counsel, the Spirit of power, the Spirit of knowledge, and the Spirit of the fear of the Lord, and make them (your enemies) flee before you seven ways. It's a set up. The enemies who dare mess with the blood washed believer, the overcomer, will have to deal with the sevenfold Holy Spirit, who is no weakling at all. It is with this purpose in mind that we now turn to a closer look into the *Seven Levels of Promise for the Overcomer.*

Notes For The Overcomer

CHAPTER FOUR

Seven Beatitudes and

Hymns of Praise in the

Book of The Revelation

Beatitudes are blessings of great depth, meaning, and content. The Book of Revelation contains seven beatitudes:

1) Revelation 1:3:

"Blessed is he that readeth, and they that hear the words of this prophecy, and keep those things which are written therein: for the time is at hand."

2) Revelation 14:13:

"And I heard a voice from heaven saying unto me, Write, Blessed are the dead which die in the Lord from henceforth: Yea, saith the Spirit, that they may rest from their labours; and their works do follow them ."

This particular verse is probably the most famous of all the seven blessings of Revelation. These are not "fly-by-night" blessings, but the stuff of which life, death, and life after death are made. The consolation of this verse is heard daily somewhere in the world, especially at memorials, wakes, and funerals. For two millennia, Christians have been comforted and encouraged in the knowledge that dying in the Lord leads to a blessed eternal life with Jesus. On the other hand, dying without a personal relationship with Jesus Christ leads to eternal damnation.

"Their works do follow them." All the good works performed by blood-washed, overcoming believers in Christ follow them to Heaven. Only the blood of Jesus Christ gets the Christian overcomer into Heaven, but the Christian overcomer's works do follow him or her, and speak for him or her regarding the type of crown, the level of literal responsibility in heaven and the New Jerusalem, and the other rewards he or she will receive for their labors in Christ. Our works do not save us, but God judges us as people of the way concerning our works. The song entitled "May The Works I've

Done Speak For Me" was inspired by, rooted, and grounded in Revelation 14:13.

May The Works I've Done Speak For Me

May the works I've done speak for me.

May the works (I've done) speak for me.

When I'm resting in my grave,

there's nothing more to be said;

may the works (the works I've done)

let it speak for me, (for me).

May the life I live speak for me.

May the life (I live) speak for me.

When I'm resting in my grave,

there's nothing more to be said;

may the life (the life I live)

let it speak for me, (for me).

The works I've done,

sometimes it seems so small,

it seems like I've done nothing at all.

Lord I'm (leaning) and depending on You,

if I do right You're gonna see me through;

may the works (the works I've done),

let it speak for me (for me).

Speak for me,

Speak for me.

3) Revelation 16:15:

"Behold, I come as a thief. Blessed is he that watcheth, and keepeth his garments, lest he walk naked, and they see his shame."

If our daily Christian walk does not line up with our daily Christian talk in this lifetime by being boldly empowered by God's amazing grace, then we will walk in nakedness and total shame in hell in the life to come. So let us take off the spirit of heaviness, and put on the garment of praise. Most of all, let us all keep our garments clean., keep our hearts clean, and keep our lives clean.

4) Revelation 19:9:

"And he saith unto me, Write, Blessed are they which are called unto the marriage supper of the Lamb. And he saith unto me, these are the true sayings of God."

Guess who's coming to dinner with Jesus Christ? Overcomers of every race, ethnic group, nationality, culture, and tribe who have been washed in the soul cleansing blood of the Lamb.

5) Revelation 20:6:

"Blessed and holy is he that hath part in the first resurrection: on such the second death hath no power, but they shall be priests of God and of Christ, and shall reign with him a thousand years."

Let us go up in the first load, the first resurrection. Let us be rapture ready, so the second death will have no power over us. There is no eternal damnation for the soul that is rapture ready. That believer shall reign with Jesus even in the millennium.

6) Revelation 22:7:

"Behold, I come quickly: blessed is he that keepeth the sayings of the prophecy of this book."

"He that has an ear let him hear what the Spirit says to the churches." "Even so, come, Lord Jesus." "We overcome Satan by the blood of the Lamb and the word of our testimony." All of these are sayings found in the Book of Revelation. Let us keep the sayings of the prophecy of this book.

7) Revelation 22:14:

"Blessed are they that do his commandments, that they may have right to the tree of life, and may enter in through the gates into the city."

Those who throw out the Ten Commandments—God's commandments—will never have a right to the Tree of Life, and will never enter into the gates of Heaven. When we respect and do God's commandments, we are empowered to embrace the life-changing grace of God.

Seven Hymns of Wonderful Praise and Worship in the Book of Revelation

There are seven distinct and vivid scenes of breathtaking heavenly praise and worship in the Book of Revelation. The seven hymns of the Book of Revelation existed long before great classic life-changing hymns of the church were written, hymns such as: "Holy, Holy, Holy," "Amazing Grace," "Precious Lord," "What a Fellowship," "Revive Us Again," "Marching to Zion," and "Power in the Blood". These and all other human-composed hymns are only mere faint echoes of the seven original hymns sung in Heaven.

1.) **The First Hymn:**

Worship God on the Throne--The Original, "Holy, Holy, Holy"

✝ **Revelation 4:1-8**

"After this I looked, and, behold, a door was opened in heaven: and the first voice which I heard was as it were of a trumpet talking with me; which said, Come up hither, and I will shew thee things which must be hereafter. And immediately I was in the spirit: and, behold, a throne was

set in heaven, and one sat on the throne. And he that sat was to look upon like a jasper and a sardine stone: and there was a rainbow round about the throne, in sight like unto an emerald. And round about the throne were four and twenty seats: and upon the seats I saw four and twenty elders sitting, clothed in white raiment; and they had on their heads crowns of gold. And out of the throne proceeded lightnings and thunderings and voices: and there were seven lamps of fire burning before the throne, which are the seven Spirits of God. And before the throne there was a sea of glass like unto crystal: and in the midst of the throne, and round about the throne, were four beasts full of eyes before and behind. And the first beast was like a lion, and the second beast like a calf, and the third beast had a face as a man, and the fourth beast was like a flying eagle. And the four beasts had each of them six wings about him; and they were full of eyes within: and they rest not day and night, saying, Holy, holy, holy, LORD God Almighty, which was, and is, and is to come."

✝ **"Two Wings" (inspired by Revelation 4:8)**

The Negro Spiritual entitled "Two Wings," which mentions three distinct sets of two wings to cover the face, feet, and fly to glory, six wings in other words, has a clear connection to verse 8 above.

> Two wings to cover my face.
>
> Two wings to cover my feet.
>
> Two wings to fly away to glory,
>
> So the world can't do me no harm.

Holy, Holy, Holy

The classic Christian hymn entitled "Holy, Holy, Holy" also has its deep roots of Christian inspiration and history in Revelation 4, especially verse eight. Written by Reginald Heber (1783-1826) these well-known stanzas speak specifically about the Christian doctrine of the Trinity. The phrase, "God in three persons" is a sound statement of Christian theology. "Holy, Holy, Holy" was written specifically for use on Trinity Sunday, which occurs eight weeks after Resurrection Sunday, or Easter. The majestic and heart-moving tune associated with it is named "Nicaea," after the historic Council of Nicaea, which took place in the year 325. "Nicaea" was composed by John Bacchus in 1861 specifically for Bishop Heber's text, one of over 300 hymn tunes penned by this prolific composer, most of which are still in use today. Bishop Heber's classic phraseology, "Holy, holy, holy! All the saints adore Thee" refers to the 24 Elders, which represents the 12 tribes of Israel and the 12 Apostles, as well as all the Old and New Testament Saints. This phrase, as well as the phrase, "Cherubim and seraphim falling down before Thee," clearly show that the inspiration for this great hymn is found in Revelation chapter four.

> Holy, holy, holy! Lord God Almighty!
> Early in the morning our song shall rise to Thee;
> Holy, holy, holy, merciful and mighty!
> God in three Persons, blessed Trinity!

> Holy, holy, holy! all the saints adore Thee,
> Casting down their golden crowns around the glassy sea;
> Cherubim and seraphim falling down before Thee,
> Who wert, and art, and evermore shalt be.

Holy, holy, holy! tho' the darkness hide Thee,

Tho' the eye of sinful man Thy glory may not see;

Only Thou art holy; there is none beside Thee,

Perfect in power, in love, and purity.

Holy, holy, holy! Lord God Almighty!

All Thy works shall praise Thy Name, in earth, and sky, and sea;

Holy, holy, holy; merciful and mighty!

God in three Persons, blessèd Trinity! [15]

2.)   The Second Hymn: Worship the Lamb—Worthy is the Lamb, Jesus Christ

✝ Revelation 5:8-13

"And when he had taken the book, the four beasts and four and twenty elders fell down before the Lamb, having every one of them harps, and golden vials full of odours, which are the prayers of saints. And they sung a new song, saying, Thou art worthy to take the book, and to open the seals thereof: for thou wast slain, and hast redeemed us to God by thy blood out of every kindred, and tongue, and people, and

---

[15] Holy, Holy, Holy written by Reginald Heber (1783-1826)

nation; And hast made us unto our God kings and priests: and we shall reign on the earth. And I beheld, and I heard the voice of many angels round about the throne and the beasts and the elders: and the number of them was ten thousand times ten thousand, and thousands of thousands; Saying with a loud voice, Worthy is the Lamb that was slain to receive power, and riches, and wisdom, and strength, and honour, and glory, and blessing. And every creature which is in heaven, and on the earth, and under the earth, and such as are in the sea, and all that are in them, heard I saying, Blessing, and honour, and glory, and power, be unto him that sitteth upon the throne, and unto the Lamb for ever and ever."

Please give very close attention to verse twelve of this particular hymn of the Book of Revelation. Verse 12 describes seven attributes of the Lamb (Jesus) in the heavenly worship meeting around the throne. These attributes are:

1.   Power
2.   Riches
3.   Wisdom

4. Strength

5. Honor

6. Glory

7. Blessing

The world-renowned singer, songwriter, and recording artist Twila Paris penned the timeless words of the classic song entitled, **"Lamb of God"**:

Your only Son

No sin to hide

But You have sent Him,

From Your side

To walk upon this guilty sod

And to become the Lamb of God[16]

---

[16] Twila Paris, Lamb of God, 1985 EMI Christian Music Mountain Spring Music Straightway Music

Seven Scriptural Examples of God's Stand Against Ethnic Hatred Found in the Book of Revelation

Kindred and tongue and people and nation (Rev 5:9)				
✝Rev 5:9	kindred	tongue	people	nation
✝Rev 7:9	nations	kindreds	people	tongues
✝Rev 10:11	peoples	nations	tongues	kings
✝Rev 11:9	people	kindreds	tongues	nations
✝Rev 13:7	kindreds	tongues	nations	
✝Rev 14:6	nation	kindred	tongue	people
✝Rev 17:15	peoples	multitudes	nation	tongues

These seven key scriptures found in the Book of Revelation show the good, bad, and indifferent aspects of every kindred (tribe), tongue (language), people, and nation, and clearly uncovers God's constant stand against all ethnic hatred.

The four crucial words of importance, kindred (tribe), tongue

(language), people, and nation, found in these seven key

scriptures are recorded in different order in each of the seven

separate verses. In some verses, new words such as kings and

multitudes are also introduced, but in every single case, the

bottom-line point that God desires all to discover true ethnic

empowerment only through the love of Jesus Christ, the

Ultimate Overcomer, and not through an evil alliance with the

unholy trinity of the beast, false prophet, and satan is clear.

These seven key verses concerning God's rock solid stand

against ethnic hatred runs the full spectrum from a scene of

pure heavenly worship around the throne of God with all

nations represented in Rev 5:9 to the devilish deception of

murky waters where multitudes of people have joined in a

whorish and evil alliance with the anti-christ in Rev 17:5 and

everything in between.

Christ-like Champions of True Civil and

Human Rights

The heavenly hymn of worship meeting "around the throne" of the Lamb also clearly lays the very firm foundation for the most noble and godly aspects of the racial equality, human, and civil rights movements. Please note that verse nine of Revelation chapter five makes it overwhelmingly clear that Jesus Christ, the Lamb of God, has literally redeemed *"every kindred, and tongue, and people, and nation"* with His shed blood. Remember also, that this same Jesus taught His very own disciples to pray in the model prayer, *"Thy kingdom come, Thy will be done on earth as it is in heaven."* Well, if every kindred, tongue, people and nation is literally represented in Heaven without any hint of cultural or racial hatred, and will also literally "reign on the earth" with equality in representation regardless of their culture and/or ethnicity, then every *true* Christian, every single *true* blood-washed believer, must be a godly, Christ-like champion of *true* civil and human rights in this current age. We must follow the example of Jesus Christ, the Ultimate Overcomer, so that His will might be done on earth as it is in Heaven. If we do not, then we are not Christ-like at all. The struggle for social justice, racial equality, and economic parity all over the earth continues. It is time for us to wake up. The revelation is relevant right now in this real world.

3.) **The Third Hymn: The Great Multitude—Salvation to Our God...and Unto the Lamb.**

✝ **Revelation 7:9-12**

"After this I beheld, and, lo, a great multitude, which no man could number, of all nations, and kindreds, and people, and tongues, stood before the throne, and before the Lamb, clothed with white robes, and palms in their hands; And cried with a loud voice, saying, Salvation to our God which sitteth upon the throne, and unto the Lamb. And all the angels stood round about the throne, and about the elders and the four beasts, and fell before the throne on their faces, and worshipped God, Saying, Amen: Blessing, and glory, and wisdom, and thanksgiving, and honour, and power, and might, be unto our God forever and ever. Amen."

Verse twelve of chapter seven ascribes **seven attributes to God the Father,** just as verse twelve of chapter five did to Jesus Christ, the Lamb of God:

1. Blessing
2. Glory
3. Wisdom
4. Thanksgiving
5. Honor
6. Power
7. Might

4.) The Fourth Hymn: The Seventh Trumpet

✝ Revelation 11:15-18

"And the seventh angel sounded; and there were great voices in heaven, saying, The kingdoms of this world are become the kingdoms of our Lord, and of his Christ; and he shall reign for ever and ever. And the four and twenty elders, which sat before God on their seats, fell upon their faces, and worshipped God, Saying, We give thee thanks, O LORD God Almighty, which art, and wast, and art to come; because thou hast taken to thee thy great power, and hast reigned. And the nations were angry, and thy wrath is

come, and the time of the dead, that they should be judged, and that thou shouldest give reward unto thy servants the prophets, and to the saints, and them that fear thy name, small and great; and shouldest destroy them which destroy the earth."

Hallelujah Chorus

Clearly, this Scripture was the inspiration behind the glorious "Hallelujah Chorus" in *Messiah* by George Frideric Handel. During the Christmas and Easter seasons especially, people around the world are exposed to the words of this great hymn of praise in Revelation chapter 11 as they listen to or sing Handel's masterpiece. The titles "King of kings" and "Lord of lords" also come from the Book of Revelation:

✝ **Revelation 17:14:**

"These shall make war with the Lamb, and the Lamb shall overcome them: for he is Lord of lords, and King of kings:

and they that are with him are called, and chosen, and faithful."

✟ **Revelation 19:16:**

"And he hath on his vesture and on his thigh a name written, KING OF KINGS, AND LORD OF LORDS."

✟ **The "Hallelujah Chorus" from *Messiah*, George Frideric Handel**

Hallelujah.

The kingdom of this world is become

the kingdom of our Lord,

and of His Christ

and of His Christ

And He shall reign forever and ever

And he shall reign forever and ever

And he shall reign forever and ever

And he shall reign forever and ever

King of kings forever and ever, hallelujah, hallelujah,

and Lord of lords forever and ever, hallelujah, hallelujah

King of kings forever and ever, hallelujah, hallelujah,

and Lord of lords forever and ever, hallelujah, hallelujah,

King of kings, and Lord of lords

Forever and ever, hallelujah, hallelujah, hallelujah, hallelujah,

Hallelujah.[17]

5.) The Fifth Hymn: The 144,000
✝ Revelation 14:1-3

"And I looked, and, lo, a Lamb stood on the mount Sion, and with him an hundred forty and four thousand, having his Father's name written in their foreheads. And I heard a voice from heaven, as the voice of many waters, and as the voice of a great thunder: and I heard the voice of harpers harping with their harps: And they sung as it were a new

---

[17] Hallelujah, by George Frideric Händel, public domain.

song before the throne, and before the four beasts, and the elders: and no man could learn that song but the hundred and forty and four thousand, which were redeemed from the earth."

Battle Hymn of The Republic

Julia Ward Howe, one of the most famous women of the nineteenth century, was the actual innovator of the concept of Mother's Day. Mrs. Howe also wrote the "Battle Hymn of the Republic." This classic hymn, which would be quoted many times later by the great Civil Rights leader, the Rev. Dr. Martin Luther King, Jr., was born during the American Civil War, when Mrs. Howe visited her beloved Union army camp on the Potomac River, close to Washington, D. C. Mrs. Howe heard the Union Army soldiers singing the song "John Brown's Body," and she was taken with the strong spiritually moving marching beat. The very next day she wrote the words of her now famous hymn. Kendall H. Easley stated in his passage on "Julia Howe and the Civil War" that "Mrs. Howe was familiar with chapter fourteen of Revelation. She saw in the events of her day a fulfillment of the gruesome prophecy of a horrible bloodbath between the forces of righteousness and the powers of darkness. While the Civil War may have been a preliminary shadow of what John foresaw in Revelation 14, by no means did it fulfill the prophecy. The events of our day may also be preliminary fulfillments of the prophecy. One day, however, the final consummation will come.[18]

Howe said of the morning that she wrote her classic song inspired by Revelation Chapter 14: "I awoke in the grey of the morning, and as I lay waiting for dawn, the long lines of the desired poem began to entwine themselves in my mind, and I said to myself, 'I must get up and write these verses, lest I fall asleep and forget them!' So I sprang out of bed and in the dimness found an old stump of a pen, which I remembered using the day before. I scrawled the verses almost without looking at the paper."

The "Battle Hymn of the Republic," which was inspired by the Book of Revelation, appeared in the *Atlantic Monthly* in 1862. It was sung at the funerals of world-renowned British

---

[18] Kendall H. Easley, *Holman New Testament Commentary, Revelation,* Max Anders, General Editor, (Nashville: Holman Reference, 1998), 245

statesman Sir Winston Churchill, United States Senator Robert Kennedy, and in memory of United States Presidents Ronald Reagan and Richard Nixon.

The original music to "John Brown's Body," believed to have been written by John William Steffe, has been the tune associated with the "Battle Hymn of the Republic," since its earliest days.

✝ **"Battle Hymn of the Republic" by Julia Ward Howe–Inspired by the Book of Revelation**

> Mine eyes have seen the glory of the coming of the Lord;
>
> He is trampling out the vintage where the grapes of wrath are stored;
>
> He hath loosed the fateful lightning of His terrible swift sword;
>
> His truth is marching on.
>
> Glory! Glory! Hallelujah! Glory! Glory! Hallelujah!

Glory! Glory! Hallelujah! His truth is marching on.[19]

6.) The Sixth Hymn: Victorious Over the Beast--The Songs of Moses and of the Lamb

✝ Revelation 15:2-4

"And I saw as it were a sea of glass mingled with fire: and them that had gotten the victory over the beast, and over his image, and over his mark, and over the number of his name, stand on the sea of glass, having the harps of God. And they sing the song of Moses the servant of God, and the song of the Lamb, saying, Great and marvelous are thy works, Lord God Almighty; just and true are thy ways, thou King of saints. Who shall not fear thee, O Lord, and glorify thy name? For thou only art holy: for all nations shall come and worship before thee; for thy judgments are made manifest."

Please note that verse three specifically mentions *"the song of Moses, the servant of God, and the song of the Lamb,"* which will be sung in heavenly worship, a combination of old and new. We should not and must not throw out the old hymns of

---

[19] Battle Hymn of the Republic, Julia Ward Howe

the church, and we should not and must not throw out the new songs of praise and worship. In Heaven, we will be singing the songs of Moses and the songs of the Lamb. So let us practice down here on earth. Let His will be done on earth as it is in Heaven.

7.) **The 7th Hymn - The Original Hallelujah Chorus**

✝ **Revelation 19: 1-8**

"And after these things I heard a great voice of much people in heaven, saying, Alleluia; Salvation, and glory, and honour, and power, unto the Lord our God: For true and righteous are his judgments: for he hath judged the great whore, which did corrupt the earth with her fornication, and hath avenged the blood of his servants at her hand. And again they said, Alleluia. And her smoke rose up for ever and ever. And the four and twenty elders and the four beasts fell down and worshipped God that sat on the throne, saying, Amen; Alleluia. And a voice came out of the throne, saying, Praise our God, all ye his servants, and ye that fear him, both small and great. And I heard as it were the voice of a great multitude, and as the voice of many waters, and as

the voice of mighty thunderings, saying, Alleluia: for the Lord God omnipotent reigneth. Let us be glad and rejoice, and give honour to him: for the marriage of the Lamb is come, and his wife hath made herself ready. And to her was granted that she should be arrayed in fine linen, clean and white: for the fine linen is the righteousness of saints."

Seven Hebrew Words for Praise: The Sevenfold Praise and Worship Love Language of the Overcomer

1) *HALAL*

Halal is a primary Hebrew root word for praise. Our word "hallelujah" comes from this base word. It means "to be clear, to shine, to boast, show, to rave, celebrate, to be clamorously foolish."

2) *YADAH*

Yadah is a verb with a root meaning of, "the extended hand, to throw out the hand, therefore to worship with extended hand." According to the Lexicon, the opposite meaning is "to bemoan, the wringing of the hands."

3) *TODAH*

Todah comes from the same principal root word as *yadah*, but is used more specifically. *Todah* literally means, "an extension of the hand in adoration, avowal, or acceptance." By way of application, it is apparent in the Psalms and elsewhere that it is used for thanking God for "things not yet received" as well as things already at hand.

4) *SHABACH*

Shabach means, "To shout, to address in a loud tone, to command, to triumph."

5) *BARAK*

Barak means "to kneel down, to bless God as an act of adoration."

6) *ZAMAR*

Zamar means, "To pluck the strings of an instrument, to sing, to praise; a musical word which is largely involved with joyful expressions of music with musical instruments."

7) *TEHILLAH*

Tehillah is derived from the word *halal* and means, "the singing of halals, to sing or to laud; perceived to involve music, especially singing."

The Prayers of the Saints

The Book of Revelation speaks three times of the prayers of the saints. Remember that these saints were, suffering saints. Many were martyrs of the faith.

✝ **Revelation 5:8** (emphasis added):

*"And when he had taken the book, the four beasts and four and twenty elders fell down before the Lamb, having every one of them harps, and golden vials full of odours, which are **the prayers of saints.**"*

✞**Revelation 8:3** (emphasis added):

*"And another angel came and stood at the altar, having a golden censer; and there was given unto him much incense, that he should offer it with **the prayers of all saints** upon the golden altar which was before the throne."*

✞**Revelation 8:4** (emphasis added):

*"And the smoke of the incense, which came with **the prayers of the saints**, ascended up before God out of the angel's hand."*

In 1818, James Montgomery, a strong abolitionist in the fight against slavery, and who began his seminary training at seven years old, wrote the classic stanzas of **"Prayer is the Soul's Sincere Desire."** Years later, the Rev. Montgomery called this timeless prayer hymn, "the most attractive hymn I ever wrote."

> Prayer is the soul's sincere desire,
> Unuttered or expressed;
> The motion of a hidden fire
> That trembles in the breast.

Prayer is the burden of a sigh,

The falling of a tear,

The upward glancing of an eye,

When none but God is near.

Prayer is the simplest form of speech

That infant lips can try;

Prayer the sublimest strains

That reach the Majesty on high.

Prayer is the Christian's vital breath,

The Christian's native air,

His watchword at the gates of death;

He enters Heav'n with prayer.

Prayer is the contrite sinner's voice,

Returning from his ways,

While angels in their songs rejoice

And cry, "Behold, he prays!"

The saints in prayer appear as one

In word, in deed, and mind,

While with the Father and the Son

Sweet fellowship they find.

No prayer is made by man alone;

The Holy Spirit pleads,

And Jesus, on the eternal throne,

For sinners intercedes.

O Thou by Whom we come to God,

The Life, the Truth, the Way,

The path of prayer thyself hast trod:

Lord, teach us how to pray.[20]

Seven Times of Daily Praise

In Psalm 119:164, the psalmist declared: *"Seven times a day do I praise thee because of thy righteous judgments."* We can literally use seven times of praise, seven levels of praise, and

---

[20] James Montgomery, Prayer Is The Soul's Desire, 1818

the seven words for praise continually, from the depths of our heart in word and in Christ-like deed.

Dr. Frank M. Reid III, pastor of Bethel A.M.E. Church in Baltimore, Maryland, writes of what he calls, the "seven habits of highly effective churches:

> "For many church members, Sunday morning worship is the "entertainment hour" rather than an appointed time to meet with and honor God. Churches that have been restored and renewed, however, have their hearts and focus in the right place where worship is concerned. These churches practice what we could call the "seven habits of highly effective churches": the worship of God, the Word of God, the will of God, the work of God, the witness to God, the wealth of God, and the warfare of God. Worship is first because it is the most essential, yet least understood and practiced habit of all. It is the core around which everything else is built."[21]

Whether it is the seven hymns of praise and worship found in the Book of Revelation, the seven Hebrew words for praise,

---

[21] Dr. Frank M. Reid, III, *Restoring The House of God – A Plea for Radical Reformation*, (Shippensburg, PA: Treasure House, 2000), 118.

or the seven habits of highly effective churches, the revelation is certainly relevant in the area of praise and worship.

Seven is an extremely important number in the Bible and in nature as well. There are seven colors in the rainbow: red, orange, yellow, green, blue, indigo and violet.

In the field of music there are seven notes on the standard music scale: C, D, E, F, G, A and B, and they can be labeled 1, 2, 3, 4, 5, 6 and 7. In addition, the scale degrees of the traditional major scale can also be named using these terms: tonic, supertonic, mediant, subdominant, dominant, submediant, and leading tone. In the major scale, there are seven solfege syllables: do (or ut), re, mi, fa, so (or sol), la, and ti (or si).

There are seven openings in the head: two eyes, two ears, two nostrils, and a mouth. The revelation is relevant even down to the human body itself. There is no running from it. This is the fingerprint of God.

The Seven Principles of Kwanzaa

Kwanzaa

Kwanzaa is a seven-day holiday, a week-long African American festival (December 26-January 1) that concludes one year and begins another. The seven principles of Kwanzaa are:

1) *Umoja* - Unity.
Psalm 133:1:

"Behold, how good and how pleasant it is for brethren to dwell together in unity!"

2) Kujichagulia - Self-determination.
Acts 11:29:

"Then the disciples, every man according to his ability, determined to send relief unto the brethren which dwelt in Judea."

3) Ujima - Collective work and responsibility.

Leviticus 23:3:

"Six days shall work be done: but the seventh day is the Sabbath of rest, an holy convocation; ye shall do no work therein: it is the Sabbath of the Lord in all your dwellings."

4) Ujamaa - Collective economics.

Romans 12:11:

"Not slothful in business; fervent in spirit; serving the Lord."

5) Nia - Purpose.

Romans 8:28:

"And we know that all things work together for good to them that love God, to them who are the called according to his purpose."

6) Kuumba - Creativity.

Genesis 1:27:

"So God created man in his own image, in the image of God created he him; male and female created he them."

7) Imani - Faith.

Hebrews 11:1:

"Now faith is the substance of things hoped for, the evidence of things not seen."

As we can see, the revelation of seven is relevant even in culture.

The Revelation is Relevant in the Solar System, "from Sea to Shining Sea", and in History

There are seven stellar objects in the solar system that are visible to the naked eye: the sun, the moon, Mars, Mercury, Jupiter, Venus, and Saturn.

By now it should be clear that seven is a significant number not only in the Bible. It is not just that Elijah told Naaman to go and dip in the Jordan seven times; it is not just that after Jesus took seven loaves (and a few small fish), and fed the 4000, that they had seven baskets left over. It is all of those things that are very significant in the various stories in the Bible where we see the number seven pop up.

Therefore, it is not just that the Book of Revelation is outlined—the whole outline of the Book of Revelation as I presented earlier is based on the sevens. We can take the sevens that are mentioned in the Book of Revelation and literally get the chapter and verse outline from the beginning of the book until the end of the book. Only God could do that; it is supernatural, and not just in the Bible.

This message of *Seven Levels of Promise for the Overcomer* is evident with the seven seas and the seven oceans of the world.

The seven seas:

1. Adriatic Sea
2. Aegean Sea
3. Arabian Sea
4. Black Sea
5. Caspian Sea
6. Mediterranean Sea
7. Red Sea.

The seven oceans in the world:

1. North Pacific Ocean

2. South Pacific Ocean

3. North Atlantic Ocean

4. South Atlantic Ocean

5. Indian Ocean

6. Southern Ocean

7. Arctic Ocean

Whether on land or sea, whenever we look at this message of *Seven Levels of Promise for the Overcomer*, we can be confident that God is telling us something important.

Not only do the seven seas and the seven oceans and the seven colors in the rainbow point to the glory of God, but the sun itself has connections to the number seven. In a powerful complement to the message of *Seven Levels of Promise for the Overcomer*, the sun declares daily seven clear pictures of our Lord and Savior, Jesus Christ.

1. The sun is God's great fountain natural of light, and Jesus Christ, is the supernatural light of the whole wide world. He is the Son of God who rises with healing in His wings. Jesus gave supernatural light on the first day of creation, long before God placed the

sun and the moon in the sky on the fourth day of creation. The revelation is relevant.

2. The sun is the natural ruler of the day, which points ultimately to the sovereignty of the Lord Jesus Christ.

3. The sun is the cause of life, which points to the life of Christ

(see John 1:4).

4. The sun is the natural source of heat, which points to the supernatural love of Christ (see Luke 24:32).

5. The sun is God's natural bestower of color, which represents the supernatural grace of Christ (see Isaiah 35:1-2).

6. The sun is God's awesome natural power of attraction, which points to the supernatural power of Christ (see John 22:39).

7. The sun is God's daily natural dispenser of blessing, which points to the supernatural blessings of Christ (see Psalm 134:11).

Even the common lowly ladybug has seven spots on its back. The vast majority of mammals on the earth have seven vertebrae in their necks.

Seven is not a magic number, but it is a significant number. Even the key elements of good health point to the *Seven Levels of Promise for the Overcomer,* These are very relevant considering the fact that our body is the temple of the Holy Spirit. In his book entitled, *The Seven Pillars of Health - The Natural Way To Better Health For Life,* Dr. Don Colbert clearly points out that these not seven "fads" of health, or seven "theories" of health, but **seven "pillars" of health**. In other words, they are the critical foundation upon which good health rests. They are:

Pillar 1—Water

Pillar 2—Sleep and Rest

Pillar 3—Living Food

Pillar 4—Exercise

Pillar 5—Detoxification

Pillar 6—Nutritional Supplements

Pillar 7—Coping With Stress

There are also seven wonders of the ancient world:

1) **The Great Pyramid of Giza,** near the ancient city of Memphis, which served as a tomb for the Egyptian Pharaoh Khufu.

2) **The Hanging Gardens of Babylon,** a legendary palace on the banks of the Euphrates river, built by King Nebuchadnezzar II, the same Babylonian king mentioned in the Old Testament Book of Daniel.

3) **An enormous statue of Zeus,** "king" of all the gods in the Greek pantheon, carved by the great sculptor Pheidias. Pagan idols such as this testify to the genuine but misguided spiritual hunger of mankind. Early Christians had to contend daily with the reality of pagan worship. It was a thorny problem for the church of that day because many converts to Christ came out of just such a lifestyle, and faced the constant danger of falling back into their old pagan ways of thinking and worship. Peter, Paul, James, and John all dealt with this reality and its dangers in their New Testament letters.

4) **The Temple of Artemis,** at Ephesus. Artemis was the Greek goddess of hunting and wild nature, and Ephesus was the center of her worship cult. Christians of the church in Ephesus lived with the daily reality of idol worship at the Temple of Artemis, which included acts of "sacred prostitution." Such moral depravity was a constant

challenge and source of temptation to the Ephesian Christians, which may be one reason the Lord called them to account for leaving their first love for Him, and appealed to them to return (Rev. 2:1-7).

5) **The Mausoleum at Halicarnassus,** a fascinating tomb constructed for King Maussollos, Persian satrap of Caria.

6) **The Colossus of Rhodes,** an enormous statue of Helios, the sun god, erected by the Greeks in 288 BC at the entrance to the harbor of the Mediterranean island of Rhodes. The 105-foot-tall statue stood with one foot on either side of the harbor entrance.

7) **The Lighthouse of Alexandria,** built by the Ptolemies on the island of Pharos, just off the coast of Alexandria, their capital city.

Notes For The Overcomer

CHAPTER FIVE

The Seven Churches of

Asia Minor

T
he seven churches addressed by Christ in chapters two and three of the Book of Revelation were seven literal churches—seven active and full-fledged congregations in seven cities located in what is today western Turkey. These early Christian congregations endured much hardship and persecution during the most oppressive era of the Roman Empire. Although none of these churches (or their cities) have continued into the modern era, archaeological remains of all seven locations have been found and excavated.

These seven ancient cities prospered because of their close proximity to the Aegean Sea to the west, as well as the major trade routes between the West and the East. Trade and traffic from all the known world passed through these cities, making them major cultural hubs as well. It was only natural that Christian churches would arise early on in these cosmopolitan centers.

Each of the seven churches had distinctive characteristics and personalities that are revealed in the brief letters John wrote to them under Christ's direction:

1. **Ephesus** – The Loveless Church—The desirable church that left its first love (Revelation 2:1-7). Once the influential capital city of Asia Minor, with a large harbor on the Aegean Sea, Ephesus today, is an abandoned ruin of ancient streets, pillars, and arches.

2. **Smyrna** – The Suffering Church—The persecuted church that suffered poverty and martyrdom (Revelation 2:8-11). Located north of Ephesus in a powerful trading position on the Aegean Sea, Smyrna was known for its harbors, commerce, and marketplaces. The primary ruins of Smyrna are located in the modern Turkish city of Izmir.

3. **Pergamum** (Pergamos) – The Worldly Church—The church that mixed pagan and Christian doctrines and needed to repent (Revelation 2:12-17). Pergamum was located on the plains and foothills along the Caicus River. It was considered a major city in Asia Minor from

the 3rd century B.C. onward, and became a hub for both Greek and Roman temple worship.

4. **Thyatira** – The False Church—The church that followed a seductive prophetess (Revelation 2:18-29). Located about 42 miles inland from the Aegean Sea, Thyatira was known for its textiles and dyeing trade. Today, it is the Turkish city of Akhisar.

5. **Sardis** – The "Dead" Church—The church that fell asleep (Revelation 3:1-6). Sardis was situated on the banks of the Pactolus River, 60 miles inland from Ephesus and Smyrna. Popular ruins today include the decadent temples and bathhouse complexes.

6. **Philadelphia** – The Persevering Church—The church that endured patiently (Revelation 3:7-13). Philadelphia, whose name means "City of brotherly love," was located on the Cogamis River, about 80 miles east of Smyrna. Like Pergamum, Philadelphia was known for its variety of temples and worship centers.

7. **Laodicea** – The "Lukewarm" Church—The church with a faith that was neither hot nor cold (Revelation 3:14-22). Laodicea was located in the Lycus River Valley of western Asia Minor, a primary trade route between the

cultures of the West and East. The city was known as a primary hub for the Roman aqueduct system.

Map of the Seven Churches of Asia Minor

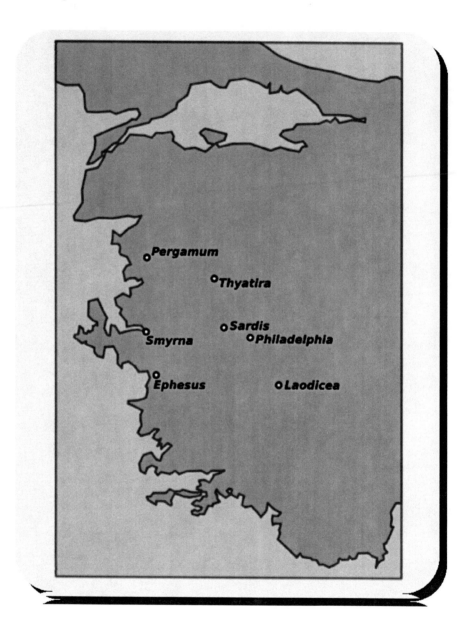

Seven Churches of Asia Minor in the Book of Revelation – Their Ultimate Significance

The seven churches of Asia Minor in Revelation are literal churches from the first century A.D. However, the seven churches in Revelation also have spiritual significance for churches and believers today. Indeed, the primary purpose for John writing his letters to the seven churches was to deliver Christ's "report card" for the churches of that time. However, a second purpose for John's inspired writings was to describe seven types of churches (and individual believers) that would surface repeatedly throughout history. These short letters to the seven churches of Revelation act as quick and poignant reminders to all who call themselves "followers of Christ."

1) The Church of Ephesus—The Loveless Church (Revelation 2:1-7)

Christ begins His address to the church at Ephesus by identifying Himself as the one *"that holdeth the seven stars (pastors) in his right hand, who walketh in the midst of the seven golden candlesticks (churches)"* (Revelation 2:1b). He then commends the church for their labor, patience, perseverance, and refusal to tolerate evil people and false prophets in their midst. Nevertheless, He rebukes them for leaving their first love (for Him), and counsels them to *"repent and do the first works"* (Revelation 2:4b), lest He come and remove their candlestick from its place.

Historically, we know that the apostles, John and Paul, had a tremendous impact upon the church at Ephesus. John is believed to have had an extensive ministry in Ephesus, while Paul's letter to the Ephesians, as well as the references in the Book of Acts to his Ephesian ministry, reveal the depth of his influence there. Aquila and Priscilla, fellow tentmakers with Paul, as well as his co-laborers in the Gospel, were a husband and wife ministry team who hosted a church in their house and ministered in Ephesus. Paul's son in the ministry, Timothy, whom he mentored, also pastored the saints at Ephesus. In spite of this extensive apostolic ministry spanning many years, by the end of the first century, the church at Ephesus had lost their first love, and were in deep need of genuine revival.

After rebuking the Ephesians for the loss of their first love and appealing to them to repent, Christ offers a great promise to those who prove faithful—to those who repent and return to their first love: *"To him that overcometh will I give to eat of the tree of life, which is in the midst of the paradise of God"* (Revelation 2:7b). This is a very important promise. All of us should desire to eat of the Tree of Life, because *"the leaves of the tree [are] for the healing of the nations"* (Revelation 22:2b). And the nations certainly need healing today. So even though it was addressed to a church of the first century, this message to Ephesus contains principles that are timeless and apply to us today. That should motivate us to deal positively with the pain, the pressure, the problems, and the predicaments and difficulties that life dishes out to us every day.

2) The Church of Smyrna—The Suffering Church (Revelation 2:8-11)

The persecuted church of Smyrna received no rebuke from Christ, because they were faithful in the midst of suffering and He found no fault in them. Instead, He commended them for their faithfulness despite their trials, and for their poverty (though they were spiritually rich). He acknowledged that more persecution was coming, but encouraged them to *"Fear none of those things which thou shalt suffer,"* because their suffering would be of limited duration, but those who were *"faithful unto death"* would be given a *"crown of life"* (Revelation 2:10). He also promised that *"He that overcometh shall not be hurt of the second death"* (Revelation 2:11).

What a powerful statement, that those who overcome will not be hurt by the second death! In other words, if our hearts are right with God, when we die the first time—physical death—we will hear God say to us in the time of judgment: *"Well done, good and faithful servant...enter thou into the joy of thy lord"* (Matthew 25:21). Those who face the second death (spiritual death) will hear instead: *"Depart from me, ye that work iniquity"* (Matthew 7:23b). If we are "rapture ready," we will not be hurt in the second death. For us, that day will be a time of great restoration, a time of resurrection, a time of elevation to the fullness of our destiny in Christ. The classic poem "Measure of A Man" points to the godly-man who will not be hurt in the second death.

MEASURE OF A MAN

Not - How did he die? But - How did he live?

Not - What did he gain? But - What did he give?

These are the things that measure the worth

Of a man as a man, regardless of birth.

Not - What was his station? But - had he a heart?

And - How did he play his God-given part?

Was he ever ready with a word of good cheer

To bring back a smile, to banish a tear?

Not - What was his church? Not - What was his creed?

But - Had he befriended those really in need?

Not - What did the sketch in the newspaper say?

But - How many were sorry when he passed away?

These are the things that measure the worth

Of a man, as a man, regardless of birth.

3) The Church of Pergamos—The Compromising Church (Revelation 2:12-17)

Christ identified Himself to the church of Pergamos as the one who held a sharp, two-edged sword. This church held many faithful and persevering believers who held true to Christ even though they were living in a city where "Satan's seat" was. However, the church also had made some compromises with the pagan world, and it was here that Christ found fault with them. Specifically, they tolerated in their midst, people who

156

held to the practices of Balaam and the Nicolaitans' pagan doctrines and customs of worship that involved idolatry and gross sexual immorality including wild orgies and pagan feasts. Christ warned them to repent of their compromise and tolerance of evil, or else He would come to them quickly and fight against them with the sword of His mouth. To the overcomer, however, He promised to *"give to eat of the hidden manna,"* and to *"give him a white stone"* with a name written on it that only that person would know (Revelation 2:17).

4) The Church of Thyatira—The Corrupt Church (Revelation 2:18-29)

Like the other three preceding churches, the church of Thyatira had many faithful believers, and Christ knew and commended their works, charity, service, faith and patience. He identified Himself to them as *"the Son of God, who hath his eyes like unto a flame of fire, and his feet are like fine brass"* (Revelation 2:18). In other words, His eyes were all-seeing, and He could see into the very depths of their spirit. Their fault lay in the fact that they had allowed themselves to become corrupted by the presence of an influential false prophet, symbolically referred to as Jezebel, the evil and pagan wife of

Israel's King Ahab, who had seduced many church members into idolatry with its false worship and sexual immorality. Having passed through a period of grace unrepentant, this "Jezebel" now faced the Lord's judgment, along with all of her idolatrous "children" (Revelation 2:22-23). To those who have remained true, however, He says, *"I will put upon you none other burden...hold fast till I come"* (Revelation 2:24-25).

Christ's promise to the overcomers in Thyatira is twofold: He will give them *"power over the nations,"* and He will give them the *"morning star"* (Revelation 2:26-28). They will be able to go and minister anywhere, because they have endured so much persecution and yet remained faithful. They will have the ability to go into any culture and minister and make a difference.

In addition, they will also know Christ as the Morning Star. After enduring so much darkness, they will recognize Him as the One who shines so brightly in bringing them through, and in giving them rest. This promise is the same for all believers who overcome in every age, including ours.

5) The Church of Sardis—The Dead Church (Revelation 3:1-6)

To this church Christ described Himself as the one who has *"the seven Spirits of God, and the seven stars"* (Revelation 3:1). Although the church in Sardis has a "name" or reputation of being alive, it is in truth a dead church. There are a few in the church who have not *"defiled their garments,"* and He promises that those few will *"walk with me in white: for they are worthy"* (Revelation 3:4). His charge to them is to *"Be watchful, and strengthen the things which remain, that are ready to die"* (Revelation 3:2). In every church, even churches that by and large are not following the will of God, there are always a few believers who want to serve the Lord. It is important to strengthen those few, because they can be the key to turning the whole church around. As they learn to let the Lord work through them, Holy Ghost fire can ignite and transform the entire church.

Christ counsels them to hold fast, repent, and be watchful, otherwise He will come upon them unexpectedly, like a thief. The Bible says that the Lord will come like a thief in the night, especially for those who are not ready, but for those of us who are ready, even though we may not know the day or the hour, we will have a sense in our spirit that we are in a season where we need to be ready. We know the Lord is coming back, so what should we do in the meantime?

Live holy, stay busy with the Lord's business, and occupy until He comes, so that when He comes, He will find us faithful, ready, and true.

The great promise Christ gives here is that the overcomer *"shall be clothed in white raiment; and I will not blot out his name out of the book of life, but I will confess his name before my Father, and before his angels"* (Revelation 3:5).

6) The Church of Philadelphia—The Faithful Church (Revelation 3:7-13)

To the church of Philadelphia, Jesus Christ, the Ultimate Overcomer, identified Himself as the One Who is holy and true and Who holds the keys of David. Jesus opens the door that no man can shut, and shuts the door that no man can open. Like the church in Smyrna, the church in Philadelphia receives no criticism from the Lord because He finds no fault in them. He knows their works. He has set before them an open door that no man can shut—a wide-open opportunity for ministry and influence. Because they have a "little strength", have kept His Word and have not denied His name, even in the face of persecution and opposition, Jesus promises to preserve them from the *"hour of temptation, which shall come upon all the world"* (Revelation 3:10). He encourages them to hold fast, because He is coming quickly. As for the overcomer, *"Him that overcometh will I make a pillar in the temple of my God...write upon him the name of my God, and the name of the city of my God...and I will write upon him my new name"* (Revelation 3:12). He promises overcomers a secure and worthy place in His Father's house.

Now, dear friends, it is very important for us to remember that there were only two positive letters or messages given by Jesus Christ to the seven churches. Five of the churches, although commended for some good things, received criticism and a call to repent of their errors and failings. Only the churches in Smyrna and Philadelphia received no criticism. Theirs were the only two messages that were completely positive in nature. "Smyrna" comes from the word "myrrh," which means "suffering," and Philadelphia was the church of brotherly love.

Jesus told the church of Philadelphia that He had set before them an open door which no man can shut, and He does the same thing for believers today, He opens up doors that no man can shut, but the opening of these doors hinge on our faithfulness. If we are faithful to Him, nothing can hinder us from going through the doors He has opened. The church at Philadelphia was a faithful congregation, and the Lord opened to them unlimited opportunity.

Revelation 3:7 says: *"And to the angel of the church at Philadelphia write; These things saith he that is holy, he that is true, he that hath the key of David, he that openeth and no man shutteth, and shutteth and no man openeth."* We are dealing with a God who is aware of everything. He is holy, He is true, He has the key of David, He has the authority to open and shut, and He knows our works (Revelation 3:8).

The "open door" that Jesus sets before the Philadelphian church is a door of opportunity. There are other doors mentioned in the Scriptures, such as the door of fellowship (see Revelation 3:20 below, in relation to the church in Laodicea).

We could call these doors of opportunity doorways of destiny. Of course, Jesus Himself is the door. He is the way, the truth, and the life, and no one comes to the Father except by Him (John 14:6). So not only is Jesus the doorway to God, He is the *only* doorway.

However, there are many doors that Jesus opens in our lives, and the doors He opens, no man can shut.

Christ commended the Philadelphian Christians when He said in verse 8, *"...for thou hast a little strength."* They were not relying on their own strength, or their own ability, but on the strength of God, and this was a good thing. Furthermore, they had kept the Lord's Word and had not denied His name, even in the face of opposition and persecution. Under all circumstances they had remained faithful to God. They didn't have the strength that many of the other congregations had, they didn't have the numbers or the political prestige that many of the other congregations had, but they had kept the Word of God and had faithfully confessed Christ before men. Jesus said: *"Whosoever therefore shall confess me before men, him will I confess also before my Father which is in heaven. But whosoever shall deny me before men, him will I also deny before my Father which is in heaven"* (Matthew 10:32-33). The Christians in Philadelphia knew the blessings that come with faithful confession. A great door of opportunity lay open before them.

Continuing on to verse nine, Christ says: *"Behold I will make of them of the synagogue of Satan, which say they are Jews, and are not, but do lie; behold I will make them to come and worship before thy feet, and to know that I have loved thee."* Apparently, much of the opposition and persecution the church in Philadelphia faced came from the Jews in that city. Because of their opposition to the truth of God, Christ calls them *"the synagogue of Satan,"* meaning that they were serving the cause of the devil even as they believed they were serving God. Christ's word of comfort to the church is that the day will come when their persecutors will be brought low and made to *"come and worship before thy feet, and to know that I have loved thee."* Their victory is assured as long as they remain faithful and hold fast to their confession.

In verse ten, Christ gives another promise to the faithful Philadelphians: *"Because thou hast kept the word of my patience, I also will keep thee from the hour of temptation, which shall come upon all the world, to try them that dwell upon the earth."* What a powerful promise! Because they had *"kept the word of [His] patience,"* because they had not gotten caught up with the synagogue of Satan or climbed into bed with the spirit of Jezebel, the Lord would protect them from the time of great trial that was soon to come on the earth. They did not have many earthly resources, but they had the Redeemer; they had the Holy One on the inside.

Patience is always an important virtue, but particularly during times of trials and tribulations. As we read the Book of Revelations, we know that all of this relates to the end times, but at the same time, these are timeless principles of God's eternal Word. First of all, this Word was spoken to the church that was alive during the period of time when the apostle John was writing, long after the deaths of Christ and all the other apostles. Second, it applies to different historical periods in the church. And third, it applies to our lives today. We have to make sure that we do not have the synagogue of Satan in our personality. In our character traits, we have to make sure that: we are not in bed with the spirit of Jezebel; we are not in the seat of Satan; and we are not letting the systems of this world manipulate us, and control us, to the point where we don't make the right decisions, and where we're being led by the enemy, instead of being led by the Spirit of God.

As we remain faithful to the Lord and to His Word, He can keep us and preserve us through the "hour of temptation" that will come into the world.

And if God can preserve us during the time of great temptation and tribulation, He certainly can preserve us through the hours of temptation that we each face every day. After all, *"greater is He that is in [us], than he that is in the world"* .(1 John 4:4).

Continuing on to verse eleven, Christ says: *"Behold, I come quickly: hold that fast which thou hast, that no man take thy crown."* A crown represents a reward, and we have to hold to what God has told us and shared with us. There is a song that says, "Hold to His hands / God's unchanging hands / build your hope on things eternal / hold to God's unchanging hands."

Finally, in verse twelve Jesus issues the promise to the overcomer: *"Him that overcometh will I make a pillar in the temple of my God, and he shall go no more out: and I will write upon him the name of my God, and the name of the city of my*

God, which is new Jerusalem, which cometh down out of heaven from my God: and I will write upon him my new name." In our day we hear about "pillars of the community," that this man or this woman is a "pillar," or an important part of the support structure of the community. However, if we hold fast to the Word that God has given us, and allow no man to take our crown, we will become "pillars" in God's house, where we can cast our crowns at His feet and offer up to Him the perfect sacrifice of our praise and worship.

We do not have to wait until we get to Heaven to become a pillar in the temple of our God; we can be that today. How? By standing up for what is right when temptation and trials come, and by remaining steadfast with God. It is not always easy to be *"steadfast, unmoveable, always abounding in the work of the Lord, forasmuch as ye know that your labor is not in vain in the Lord"* (1 Corinthians 15:58), but if you do it, then you become a witness to those who did not think they would be able to make it. They say, "Well, if he can make it, if he or she was tempted by drugs, and by peer pressure, and by sex, and still came out on top, then I can too."

Our example will encourage others to submit their lives to the Lord, even if they

have not been treating their body like the

temple of God it is.

7) **The Church of Laodicea—The Lukewarm Church (Revelation 3:14-22)**

Because of its particular characteristics, the church of Laodicea is commonly related or compared to the church of today. To this church Christ identifies Himself as *"the Amen, the faithful and true witness, the beginning of the creation of God"* (Revelation 3:14). Jesus Christ is the "Amen." That is a powerful statement because "amen" means "so be it." In church we say amen when we are in agreement with the statement made by the preacher. Jesus also is *"the faithful and true witness."* Human witnesses have been known to lie, but Jesus never lies. Everything Jesus says is true; He always testifies to the truth.

As with the other churches, Jesus tells the Laodiceans, *"I know thy works."*

In other words, He says, "I know the real

deal. I know what's going on behind the

scenes, and what you're hiding from folks.

There is no way you can fool God.

Of their works He says, *"thou art neither cold nor hot: I would that thou were cold or hot."* God wants us to be one way or the other. If we are going to live for God, He wants us to live for Him—to be hot and on fire for Him. On the other hand, if we are going to be cold, He would rather we just go all the way and be cold rather than sit on the fence in the middle and pretend. We cannot straddle the fence, because Jesus searches the reigns of the heart. Jesus knows what is really going on. He knows when we are genuine and when we are being phony.

Therefore, He would rather us to be either hot and on fire for God, or cold. In addition, He goes on to say, *"So then because thou art lukewarm, and neither cold nor hot, I will spue thee out of my mouth"* (Revelation 3:16). I love to drink an ice-cold glass of water, especially on a hot day, but I do not want lukewarm water. On a cold day, I like to have some nice hot tea. However, if the tea cools to the point of being lukewarm, it is just a waste.

Lukewarmness of spirit is just as distasteful

and wasteful to God. Jesus Christ, the

ultimate Overcomer, wants us to be hot for the cause of the kingdom of heaven.

Verse seventeen cites the reason for the lukewarmness of the Laodiceans: *"Because thou sayest, I am rich, and increased in goods, and have need of nothing; and knowest not that thou art wretched, and miserable, and poor, and blind, and naked."* They were complacent, thinking they needed nothing when they really needed everything. We see this same attitude in the world today. Many of us think we have it all together, and therefore do not need God. Actually, we need God as never before. When we say that we are rich, we are actually poor. Many folks say that they have increased in goods, but it is not always those things that are good for us. When we say that we are in need of nothing, we are in need of everything; we are in need of Christ, and in need of God. In addition, when He says that we are *"wretched, and miserable, and poor, and blind, and naked,"* He is telling the truth. We could have a million dollars in the bank, yet lack peace of mind. In his book entitled, *God In The Ghetto,* the late Rev. Dr. William Augustus Jones, Jr. wrote concerning Revelation 3:15-19 that, "Lukewarm religion leaves the Church wretched, miserable, poor, blind, and naked, deserving of death but ready for redemption. And redemption always begins with repentance. When repentance does not occur, divine activity in behalf of victims is in no wise halted, for the Biblical record reveals that God is always on the side of the disinherited. He is the God of the ghetto!"[22]

Only God can give peace of mind, the peace that passes all understanding.

Christ then offers the Laodiceans wise counsel: *"I counsel thee to buy of me gold tried in the fire, that thou mayest be rich; and white raiment, that thou mayest be clothed, and that the shame of thy nakedness do not appear; and anoint thy eyes with eyesalve, that thou mayest see"* (Revelation 3:18). If we want to be rich, then our gold has to be tried in the fire. It has to be purified. God wants to purify us.

"White raiment" suggests the richness and purity of being in Christ, to cover up the shameful nakedness of our sin and rebellion against God. We have understood the shame of our nakedness and the shame of our wretchedness, the sin sick shame of our soul, but Christ has come to cleanse us, to give us

22 God In The Ghetto, William A. Jones, Jr., Progressive Baptist Publishing House, Elgin, IL, pg 61

white raiment, pure raiment to put upon us, and to cleanse us on the inside.

"Eyesalve" symbolizes the healing of spiritual blindness so that we might see again. Proverbs 29:18 says: *"Where there is no vision, the people perish."* We need to realize the wretched state of much of the church today. Peter said that judgment begins at the house of God, (1 Peter 4:17). Judgment, cleansing, and deliverance all must begin at the house of God with the people of God. We have to take that rebuke, that discipline, that correction that God gives us, so the world can begin to get back on the right course. The world will never get on the right course unless the church first gets on the right course.

The Lord's rebuke is always tempered by love: *"As many as I love, I rebuke and chasten: be zealous therefore, and repent"* (Revelation 3:19). Because God loves us, He disciplines us, but the purpose of the discipline is to bring us to repentance and to teach us how to live as holy and righteous children of God. Christ tells us to "be zealous" and repent. Zealousness involves conscious, deliberate action. We have to be zealous to repent; we have to be zealous to turn from our wicked ways. It is a choice we must make. Second Chronicles 7:14 says, *"If my people, which are called by My name, shall humble themselves, and pray, and seek my face, and turn from their wicked ways; then will I hear from heaven, and will forgive their sin, and will heal their land."*

This promise from God is conditional, however. The word "if" at the beginning indicates that there are certain things that we must do in order to satisfy the conditions upon which God will act. *If* we humble ourselves, pray, seek God's face, and repent of our wickedness, *then* God will hear, forgive, and heal.

Christ's love and longing for His wayward people are revealed in the next verse: *"Behold, I stand at the door, and knock: if any man hear my voice, and open the door, I will come in to him, and will sup with him, and he with me"* (Revelation 3:20). This is not the door of salvation, but of fellowship. He is talking here to believers, not unbelievers.

Whereas the church in Philadelphia was given a door of opportunity, the Laodiceans (and, by extension, us) are offered a door of fellowship, a door where He is saying, "Come out of religion and enter into relationship."

Christ has never called His church into religion. The only time religion is mentioned in connection with the Christian faith is when James defines *"pure religion"* as ministering to widows and orphans (James 1:27).

The fact that the Bible speaks of "pure religion" or good religion, implies that there is "bad religion". Bad religion is not practiced only by pagans and others who defy or deny the one true God, but also by many who claim to believe in and serve God. One good example of this are the scribes, Pharisees, and other Jewish religious leaders of Jesus' day, many of whom were complicit in His crucifixion. Jesus told Nicodemus, a Pharisee, *"You must be born again"* (John 3:7). This is a direct contrast to religion, because it involves relationship.

Dead religion will not get us into the kingdom of Heaven. Mundane religion will not get us into the kingdom of God. Boring, powerless religion will not give us righteousness, joy, or peace in the Holy Ghost. Religion can never transform the hearts and minds of men and women.

We need more than religion; we need a relationship with God. We must begin to move from religion to relationship.

Finally, Christ issues His promise to the overcomers at Laodicea: *"To him that overcometh will I grant to sit with me in my throne, even as I also overcame, and am set down with my Father in his throne"* (Revelation 3:21). Here is the seventh promise in the seven levels of promise to the overcomer. We cannot limit our application of these promises just to the churches to whom they were originally given, because they apply to us as well. Those who overcome will sit with Christ on His throne. In other words, the saints of God will rule with Christ in the kingdom of Heaven. That is our destiny.

With the help of Jesus Christ, we too will overcome. I Want to Be at the Meeting Around the Throne

The classic song "Be At The Meeting," which has ministered locally in churches, as well as nationally, and internationally in many venues, and made famous by the world renowned gospel quartet, the Sensational Nightingales, contains a crucial key phrase clearly inspired by the Book of Revelation, particularly with its reference to the "meeting around the throne."

✟ **"Be At The Meeting" – Inspired by the Book of Revelation**

> I want to be at the meeting
>
> I want to be at the meeting.

Don't you know now,

I want to be at the meeting.

Early, early one-morning children,

I want to be at the meeting,

When all the saints get home

Lord, after separating, Lord, the right and the wrong,

I want to be at the meeting around the throne.[23]

With these words it is easy to envision the heavenly worship meeting around the throne, with the twenty-four elders in their white robes and golden crowns all around the throne, representing the twelve tribes of Israel and the twelve Apostles—the Old and New Testament saints, the blood-washed overcomers. The twenty-four elders were seated around the throne with Jesus Christ as overcomers, because Jesus Christ was and is the classic example of the Ultimate Overcomer. Here are the pertinent Scriptures:

---

[23] Be At The Meeting, classic gospel song made famous by the gospel quartet, the Sensational Nightingales.

✠ Revelation 4:3-4:

"And he that sat was to look upon like a jasper and a sardine stone: and there was a rainbow round about the throne, in sight like unto an emerald. And round about the throne were four and twenty seats: and upon the seats I saw four and twenty elders sitting, clothed in white raiment; and they had on their heads crowns of gold."

✠ Revelation 4:6:

"And before the throne there was a sea of glass like unto crystal: and in the midst of the throne, and round about the throne, were four beasts full of eyes before and behind."

✠ Revelation 5:11:

"And I beheld, and I heard the voice of many angels round about the throne and the beasts and the elders: and the number of them was ten thousand times ten thousand, and thousands of thousands."

✠ Revelation 7:11

"And all the angels stood round about the throne, and about the elders and the four beasts, and fell before the throne on their faces, and worshipped God."

These same Scriptures remind me of another song entitled, "Heav'n, Heav'n". We need to embrace the old Negro spirituals like this one, because it is the testifying of blood-washed overcomers who will make it to Heaven and wear a robe, and receive a crown. There could be no greater honor than to hear those seven precious words from the lips of our Lord: *"Well Done Thou Good and Faithful Servant."*

✟ **"Heav'n, Heav'n" – Inspired By The Book of Revelation**

> I got a robe, you got a robe,
> All God's children got a robe.
> When I get to Heav'n gonna put in my robe,
> Gonna shout all over God's Heav'n, Heav'n, Heav'n
> Everybody talkin' about Heav'n ain't going there,
> Heav'n, Heav'n, Heav'n.
> Gonna shout all over God's Heav'n.

I got a crown, you got a crown,

All God's children got a crown.

When I get to Heav'n gonna put in my crown,

Gonna walk all over God's Heav'n, Heav'n, Heav'n

Everybody talkin' about Heav'n ain't going there,

Heav'n, Heav'n, Heav'n.

Gonna shout all over God's Heav'n.[24]

The Scriptures from the Book of Revelation that inspired these and other great songs have also inspired the formation of many Male Chorus groups that have had and still have profound impact across the nation, such as "The Revelations," founded by my uncle, the late "Gospel Joe" Williams of Roosevelt, New York.

Yes, the revelation is relevant.

It is more than mere words; it is a ministry.

It is more than mere music; it is a ministry.

---

[24] Heav'n, Heav'n, Negro Spiritual

✝ The Seven Churches of Asia Minor

The Seven Churches of Asia Minor	Commendation from Jesus Christ	Criticism from Jesus Christ	Instruction from Jesus Christ	Seven Levels of Promise for the Overcomer
Ephesus: The Loveless Church (Rev. 2:1–7)	Rejects evil, has patience, and labored and not fainted	Left their first love	Remember from where you fell, repent, and do your first works again	Eat of the Tree of Life in the midst of the paradise of God
Smyrna: The Suffering Church (Rev. 2:8–11)	Tribulations and poverty (but rich)	None	Be faithful until death	Receive the crown of life. Not hurt in the second death
Pergamos: The Compromising Church (Rev. 2:12–17)	Held fast Christ's name and did not deny the faith	Doctrine of Balaam, idols, fornication	Repent or Christ will come quick and fight	Hidden manna and a white stone with a new name
Thyatira: The Corrupt Church (Rev. 2:18–29)	Charity, service, faith, and patience. Last more than first	Allowing the Jezebel spirit-sinful compromise	Hold fast till I come	Rule over nations and receive the morning star
Sardis: The Dead Church (Rev. 3:1–6)	Had a name for living	Was a dead church	Be watchful. Strengthen that which remains	Clothed in white raiment. Name not blotted out of the Book of Life
Philadelphia: The Faithful Church (Rev. 3:7–13)	Open door. Little strength, kept Christ's word and name	None	Hold fast so no man takes your crown	Pillar in the temple of my God, new name, & New Jerusalem
Laodicea: The Lukewarm Church (Rev. 3:14–22)	None	Not cold or hot - lukewarm	Be zealous and repent	Seated with Christ in His throne.

180

Notes For The Overcomer

CHAPTER SIX

Jesus Christ, the Ultimate Overcomer

The Garden of Gethsemane

Jesus, the Ultimate Overcomer, sweat drops of blood in the Garden of Gethsemane. When Adam ate of the forbidden fruit in the Garden of Eden, humanity fell into the cesspool of sin. As Jesus prayed in the Garden of Gethsemane concerning His fast approaching death, the agony in His heart was so great that blood oozed from His pores. Peter, James, and John were a little distance away, sleeping, despite Jesus' request that they stay awake with Him and watch and pray. A little later, Jesus was betrayed by Judas for 30 pieces of silver. During the mob's attempt to arrest Jesus, Peter cut off the ear of a slave of the high priest, but Jesus healed the man. Even as the soldiers carried Jesus away for trial, He had already begun shedding blood for us. The soil of the Garden of

Gethsemane on the Mount of Olives caught the first precious drops of our Savior's blood.

The Whipping Post

After an illegal mock trial in the middle of the night, from which He was hauled from judgment hall to judgment hall and subjected to much ridicule, Jesus was tied to a whipping post and flogged with a Roman cat of nine tails, with the ends studded with sharp pieces of metal, stone, and bone. This scourging literally tore the skin off His back. Jesus was beaten and brutalized, enduring extreme torment and torture. Prisoners often died before receiving all 39 lashes, which represented every known disease upon the face of the earth, but not Jesus. He lived, even as He shed His blood for us the second time.

The Crown of Thorns

As the Roman soldiers pressed the crown of thorns upon Jesus' head, His blood began streaming down His face. This was the third time Jesus bled on our behalf. His crown of thorns reminds us of the curse that came upon Adam to have to work the ground amongst the thorns and thistles.

His Right Hand

Having sweat drops of blood, having had His back ripped to the bone by whips, and His head lacerated by sharp thorns, Jesus carried His own cross to Golgotha, the "place of the skull," where He was crucified. He was laid on the cross, His arms stretched out along the crossbeam, and a large spike driven through His right hand. It is here that He shed his blood for the fourth time.

His Left Hand

After nailing His right hand, the Roman soldiers drove a spike through His left hand. Jesus' blood flowed for the fifth time.

His Feet

To secure Jesus properly on the cross, a third large spike was driven through both feet into the rough wood of that cross. As Jesus' cross was hoisted into place, His blood flowed down for us a sixth time.

His Side

The seventh time Jesus, the Ultimate Overcomer, shed His blood for us was after He was dead. A Roman soldier pierced His side with a spear and blood and water poured out. Blood represents redemption for all humanity, which Christ won through His death and resurrection. Water represents the Holy Spirit, signifying the birth of the Church.

Jesus said in Revelation 3:21, *"To him that overcometh will I grant to sit with me in my throne, even as I also overcame, and am set down with my Father in his throne."* If we are going to become overcomers ourselves, then we have to look at the way that Jesus, the Son of God, overcame, and pattern our lives after His life. He overcame through His life, death, and resurrection.

Rosa Parks – A True Overcomer

Sit Down Servant – Rosa Sat Down So We Could Stand Up

> Rosa Parks, a true overcomer, followed a sit down strategy so the struggle for freedom could stand up worldwide.

Rosa Parks, regarded by many as the mother of the civil rights movement, was a true overcomer. She lived out the meaning of the old spiritual, "Sit Down Servant".

Most historians date the beginning of the modern civil rights movement in the United States to December 1, 1955. That was the day when an unknown hard working seamstress in Montgomery, Alabama, refused to give up her bus seat to a white passenger. Mrs. Parks said of her historic act of civil disobedience that "I didn't want to pay my fare and then go around the back door, because many times, even if you did that, you might not get on the bus at all. They'd probably shut the door, drive off, and leave you standing there."[25] Like Rosa Parks, we too, must catch the vision of victory over hatred, racism, and sexism. Rosa Parks was arrested and fined for violating a city ordinance, but her lonely act of defiance began a major movement that ended legal segregation in America, and made her an inspiration to freedom-loving people everywhere. Mrs. Parks said of her life and legacy: "I would like to be remembered as a person who wanted to be free... so other people would be also free."[26] This soft-spoken but powerful servant of God sat down so truth and justice could stand up through her example and living testimony. Rosa Parks' sitting down was a God-given strategy to literally cause the masses to stand up for the struggle of equality. Rosa Parks once stated that, "I have learned over the years that when one's mind is made up, this diminishes fear; knowing what must be done does away with fear."[27]

---

[25] Rosa Parks, The Mother of the Civil Rights Movement, concerning her historic act of civil disobedience.

[26] Rosa Parks, The Mother of the Civil Rights Movement, concerning her life and legacy.

[27] Rosa Parks, The Mother of the Civil Rights Movement, concerning overcoming fear.

Born Rosa Louise McCauley in Tuskegee, Alabama, on February 4, 1913, she was the daughter of Mr. James McCauley, a carpenter, and Mrs. Leona McCauley, a teacher. When she was only two, Rosa moved to her grandparents' farm in Pine Level, Alabama, with her mother and younger brother, Sylvester. At the age of 11, she enrolled in the Montgomery Industrial School for Girls, a private school founded by liberal-minded women from the northern United States. The school's philosophy of self-worth was consistent with Leona McCauley's advice to "take advantage of the opportunities, no matter how few they are."

After attending Alabama State Teachers' College, the young Rosa settled in Montgomery with her husband, Raymond Parks. The couple joined the local chapter of the NAACP and worked quietly for many years to improve the lot of African-Americans in the segregated South.

The bus incident led to the formation of the Montgomery Improvement Association, led by the young and highly esteemed pastor of the Dexter Avenue Baptist Church, Rev. Dr. Martin Luther King, Jr. The Montgomery Improvement Association called for a boycott of the city-owned bus company. The boycott lasted 382 days and brought Mrs. Rosa Parks, Dr. Martin Luther King, and their cause for truth, equality, liberty, and justice to the attention of the whole world. A landmark Supreme Court decision struck down the Montgomery ordinance under which Mrs. Parks had been fined, and outlawed racial segregation on public transportation nationwide.

In 1957, Mrs. Parks and her husband moved to Detroit, Michigan where she served on the staff of U.S. Representative John Conyers. The Southern Christian Leadership Council established an annual Rosa Parks Freedom Award in her honor. After the death of her husband in 1977, Mrs. Parks founded the Rosa and Raymond Parks Institute for Self-Development. The Institute sponsors an annual summer program for teenagers called Pathways to Freedom. The young people tour the country in buses, under adult supervision, learning the history of their country and of the civil rights movement. President Clinton presented Rosa Parks with the Presidential Medal of Freedom in 1996. She received a Congressional Gold Medal in 1999.

Mrs. Parks spent her last years living quietly in Detroit, where she died on October 24, 2005 at the age of 92. After her death, her casket was placed in the rotunda of the United States

Capitol for two days, so the nation could pay its respects to the "mother of the civil rights movement," a true servant of God, and an awesome woman of divine destiny, whose uncompromising courage has helped to transform the lives of countless millions. She was the first woman in American history to lie in state at the Capitol, an honor usually reserved for Presidents of the United States. Rosa Parks, a true overcomer, followed a sit down strategy so the struggle for freedom could stand up worldwide. Mrs. Parks stated that, "Memories of our lives, of our works and our deeds will continue in others."[28]

The classic spiritual "Sit Down Servant" picks up on this theme.

✞ **Sit Down Servant**

> Sit down, servant. Sit down.
>
> Sit down, servant. Sit down.
>
> Sit down, servant. Sit down.
>
> Sit down and rest a little while.

---

[28] Rosa Parks, Mother of the Civil Rights Movement, Memories

I know you're tired. Sit down.

I know you're tired. Sit down.

I know you're tired. Sit down.

Sit down and rest a little while.

You come a mighty long way. Sit down

You come a mighty long way. Sit down.

You come a mighty long way. Sit down.

Sit down and rest a little while.[29]

Seated with Christ Figuratively Now and Literally Later

We live in a representative republic. This means that we participate in our own governing, not by our physical presence, but through elected officials who represent us in the halls of government. For example, although I am not physically present with my US senator or congressman in Washington D.C., my state senator in Albany, NY, or my town representative at the

---

[29] Sit Down Servant, Negro Spiritual

local town hall, symbolically or *positionally* I am seated with them because they represent me. In our republic, office-holders are elected to represent the people who elected them.

In a similar way (except that He was not elected), Jesus Christ, the risen Son of God, sits at the right hand of the Father, and because He has overcome and paid the price for our sins, we who have trusted Him as Savior and Lord are seated with Him symbolically and positionally in heavenly places.

In Revelation 3:21 Jesus promised, *"To him that overcometh will I grant to sit with me in my throne, even as I also overcame, and am set down with my Father in his throne."* This verse has both a figurative and a literal fulfillment. Figuratively, it is true now, because Jesus represents us before His Father night and day. Someday, it will also be true, literally, as we depart this life and are ushered fully and completely into the Lord's presence. This is a very important truth to understand with regard to the *seven levels of promise for the overcomer.*

You may have lost your job; you may have gone through a divorce; you may have gone through a bankruptcy; you may have gone through a rape; you may have gone through a situation where people have lied on you, or have done horrible things to you, or you have done horrible things to them, but regardless of your past or present circumstances, you can overcome even as Jesus overcame. His victory can be yours if you take the reality of His life, death, and resurrection, and apply them to your own situation, declaring, "I am going to live in Christ, and live to help others. I am going to die to myself, that I might become all that God wants me to be." Once you take hold of that life, death and resurrection principle and come to know the Lord both in the power of His resurrection and in the fellowship of His sufferings, you will begin to understand the richness and blessing of the *seven levels of promise for the overcomer.*

At the conclusion of each message to the seven churches, Jesus says, *"He that hath an ear, let him hear what the Spirit saith unto the churches"* (Revelation 3:22). This is key to becoming a successful overcomer. We've got to hear what the Spirit is saying to the churches, not just what the Spirit *has* said, but also what He *is* saying to each and every one of us today. Everything the Spirit says will line up perfectly with God's Word. The Holy Spirit will never say anything that contradicts the Bible because He is God, and God never contradicts Himself. He will use the Scriptures that He inspired to challenge us and put us on the cutting edge. God can and does speak to us in many different and unique ways, but everything He says is absolutely right and always relevant. The revelation is relevant, and the classic words of the Book of Revelation are extremely relevant for us today.

As we've already seen, many old Negro spirituals were inspired by words or images from the Book of Revelation. And although it is rare to hear sermons out of Revelation (except when related to end times prophecy), much practical wisdom can be found there. For example, the great civil rights leader, the Rev. Dr. Martin Luther King, Jr., preached an extremely powerful sermon from the Book of Revelation entitled "The Dimensions of a Complete Life." At one point he states:

Many, many centuries ago, out on a lonely, obscure island called Patmos, a man by the name of John caught a vision of the New Jerusalem descending out of Heaven from God. One of the greatest glories of this new city of God that John saw was completeness. It was not partial and one-sided, but it was complete in all three of its dimensions.[30]

---

[30] The Measure of a Man: by Martin Luther King Jr., Sermon- The Dimensions of a Complete Life, Publisher: Augsburg Fortress Publishers

There are seven key Negro spirituals that point to this completeness that both the apostle John and Dr. King found in the relevancy of the Revelation of Jesus Christ for the past, present, and future. These spirituals are: "Every Time I Feel The Spirit," "Steal Away," "Great Day," "Oh Freedom," "We Shall Overcome," "Listen To The Angels Shouting," and "Walk In Jerusalem Just Like John."

This connection between Negro spirituals and the Book of Revelation is important for at least three reasons. First of all, Black History is part of American History. Second, Black History is also part of World History. Third, and most important, this particular aspect of Black History is a vital part of our Christian heritage and history. In her book entitled, *No Man Can Hinder Me: The Journey from Slavery to Emancipation through Song,* noted author, Velma Maia Thomas writes: "My people told stories, from Genesis to Revelation, with God's faithful as the main characters. They knew about Adam and Eve in the Garden, about Moses and the Red Sea. They sang of the Hebrew children and Joshua at the battle of Jericho. They could tell you about Mary, Jesus, God, and the Devil. If you stood around long enough, you'd hear a song about the blind man seeing, God troubling the water, Ezekiel seeing a wheel, Jesus being crucified and raised from the dead. If slaves couldn't read the Bible, they would memorize Biblical stories they heard and translate them into songs."[31] Let's take a closer look at each of these spirituals, the Scriptures from the Book of Revelation that inspired them, and the testimonies of three Black Americans whose overcoming lifestyles show the power of these scriptures and songs in action.

Seven Key Negro Spirituals
Based on the Book of Revelation

1) "Every Time I Feel The Spirit"

☩ **Revelation 1:9-11:**

"I John, who also am your brother, and companion in tribulation, and in the kingdom and patience of Jesus Christ, was in the isle that is called Patmos, for the word of God, and for the testimony of Jesus Christ. I was in the Spirit on

---

[31] Velma Maia Thomas, No Man Can Hinder Me: The Journey from Slavery to Emancipation through Song (New York: Crown Publishers, 2001), 14

the Lord's day, and heard behind me a great voice, as of a trumpet, Saying, I am Alpha and Omega, the first and the last: and, What thou seest, write in a book, and send it unto the seven churches which are in Asia; unto Ephesus, and unto Smyrna, and unto Pergamos, and unto Thyatira, and unto Sardis, and unto Philadelphia, and unto Laodicea."

✞ **"Every Time I Feel The Spirit" – Inspired by the Book of Revelation**

Every time I feel the Spirit moving in my heart, I will pray.

Upon the mountain my Lord spoke, Out His mouth came fire and smoke.

All around me looks so fine, Ask my Lord if all was mine.

Jordan River is chilly and cold, chills the body but not the soul.

Ain't but one train on dis track, Runs to heaven and right back.[32]

---

[32] Every Time I Feel The Spirit, Negro Spiritual

The Overcoming Testimony of Marian Anderson

Marian Anderson made history as she sang with the spirit of excellence on the Lord's Day, Easter Sunday, 1939. Seventy-five thousand people turned out on the National Mall of our nation's capital to hear this phenomenal musician and woman of God sing songs of freedom.

Whenever I think of the song, "Every Time I Feel The Spirit," I am reminded of the world-renowned contralto, Marian Anderson. Born in Philadelphia in 1902, Marian began singing in the church choir as soon as she was old enough. By the time she was in her teens, it was obvious to many that God had endowed her with an especially gifted voice. Marian's church showed their encouragement and support by helping to pay for her voice lessons. Many remarked how Marian's singing style sounded like an angel on the Lord's Day. Because of her legacy of strong Christian faith, Marian Anderson had the right spirit to sing the songs that would touch the masses.

Eventually, Marian left her beloved home of Philadelphia and moved to the next level in the spirit of song by receiving formal vocal training. Following this, she embarked on a European tour that brought her captivating spirit of excellence in song to the big theaters. By 1935 she was a big star in Europe, and well on her way to becoming one of the greatest and most admired and respected singers in the world.

When this world-renowned singer was asked to perform in our nation's capital, Washington, DC, racism reared its ugly head. Originally slated to perform in Constitution Hall, she was denied access to that venue because she was black. The racists behind this action did not have the revelation of Jesus Christ, who has a heart for all ethnic groups and nationalities. One bold man defied the racists and declared, "She will sing at the Lincoln Memorial!" And indeed, Marian Anderson made history as she sang with the spirit of excellence on the Lord's Day, Easter Sunday, 1939. Seventy-five thousand people turned out on the National Mall of our nation's capital to hear this phenomenal musician and woman of God sing songs of freedom. That day, Marian Anderson's voice of victory was heard around the world.

2) "Steal Away"

✝ **Revelation 1:10:**

"I was in the Spirit on the Lord's Day, and heard behind me a great voice, as of a trumpet."

The key phrase, "The trumpet sounds with in-a my soul" clearly shows that the spiritual, "Steal Away," was inspired by Revelation 1:10. John was imprisoned on the island of Patmos when he "stole away" in the Spirit on the Lord's Day. The revelation he received that day was relevant not only to him and the people of that century, but also to people of every other century, including African slaves in America. It was relevant to the civil rights movement, and remains just as relevant today.

✝ **"Steal Away" – Inspired by the Book of Revelation**

> Steal away, steal away steal away to Jesus;
>
> Steal away, steal away home.
>
> I ain't got long to stay here.
>
> My Lord He calls me,
>
> He calls me by the thunder.
>
> The trumpet sounds with in a my soul,
>
> I ain't got long to stay here.

Green trees are bending, poor sinner stands a-tremblin,'

The trumpet sounds with in a my soul,

I ain't got long to stay here.[33]

The Overcoming Testimony of Harriet Tubman

Harriet Tubman was a true visionary leader, and an overcomer, who knew how to "steal away" to Jesus, and, like Moses of old, she knew how to rescue her people from slavery.

Hearing the spiritual "Steal Away" always makes me think of Harriet Tubman. No one really knows Harriet Tubman's date of birth, because birth records for slaves often were not properly kept. As best we know, she was born in Maryland somewhere around 1820. While she was growing up, Harriet was beaten frequently by her master. She was a hardy soul, extremely strong in spirit, soul, and body, who worked just as hard in the fields as her male counterparts. When she learned as a young woman that her brutal slave master was preparing to

---

[33] Steal Away, Negro Spiritual

sell her, she made up her mind to "steal away." One night she ran away, and succeeded in escaping to freedom in the north.

Before long, Harriet Tubman began to be known as "Moses" because she devoted the rest of her life helping other slaves to overcome their situation and "steal away" to freedom. In this cause she proved both tireless and fearless, and was one of the most successful of all the "conductors" on the Underground Railroad. Harriet saw her work as a vital (and extremely dangerous) assignment from God, but she never backed away or flinched, because she was not just a survivor but also an overcomer who cared for the oppressed.

On this Underground Railroad, Harriet's "trains" were old wagons, and her "tracks," dirt roads. Her safety stations were private homes, and her destination the "Promised Land" of freedom. **Runaway slaves on their way to freedom loved to hear Harriet sing:**

> Go down, Moses,
>
> Way down in Egypt land.
>
> Tell old Pharaoh
>
> Let my people go.[34]

---

[34] Let My People Go, Negro Spiritual

All in all, Harriet Tubman, the "Moses" of her people, helped over 300 slaves steal away successfully from slavery in the south to freedom in the north. She personally led nineteen trips herself, continually and willingly running the risk of being recaptured or killed. In fact, she eventually had a $40,000 bounty on her head, placed by unified slave owners who wanted her dead or alive! Harriet Tubman was a true visionary leader, an overcomer who knew how to "steal away" to Jesus, and, like Moses of old, she knew how to rescue her people from slavery.

3) "We Shall Overcome"

Although the composer of the tune to this classic "anthem" of the civil rights movement is unknown, the lyrics were derived from Charles Tindley's gospel song, "I'll Overcome Some Day" (1900). The connection of this song to the Book of Revelation is undeniable, particularly when we understand that overcoming is a major theme of the book. Aside from the seven references in relation to the seven churches in chapters 2 and 3, the word "overcome" or "overcometh" appears four additional times in the book (11:7; 13:7; 17:14; 21:7). Concerning the messages to the seven churches, Warren W. Wiersbe writes, "Each of these messages to the churches ends with a promise to the overcomers. These overcomers are not an elite group in the church but true believers who have trusted Christ (1John 5:1-5)."[35]

Before we proceed to the song itself, it would be appropriate here to quickly review the seven promises to the overcomer that Jesus gave to the seven churches in Asia Minor. Read these Scriptures and let them change your life!

Seven Levels of Promise for the Overcomer

✟ **Revelation 2:7b:**

"To him that overcometh will I give to eat of the tree of life, which is in the midst of the paradise of God."

✟ **Revelation 2:11b:**

"He that overcometh shall not be hurt of the second death."

✟ **Revelation 2:17b:**

"To him that overcometh will I give to eat of the hidden manna, and will give him a white stone, and in the stone a

---

[35] Warren W. Wiersbe, *With the Word – The Chapter-by-Chapter Handbook*, (Nashville: Thomas Nelson Publishers, 1991), 849.

*new name written, which no man knoweth saving he that
receiveth it."*

✝ Revelation 2:26-28:

*"And he that overcometh, and keepeth my works unto the
end, to him will I give power over the nations: And he shall
rule them with a rod of iron; as the vessels of a potter shall
they be broken to shivers: even as I received of my Father.
And I will give him the morning star."*

✝ Revelation 3:5:

*"He that overcometh, the same shall be clothed in white
raiment; and I will not blot out his name out of the book of
life, but I will confess his name before my Father, and before
his angels."*

✝ Revelation 3:12:

*"Him that overcometh will I make a pillar in the temple of
my God, and he shall go no more out: and I will write upon
him the name of my God, and the name of the city of my
God, which is new Jerusalem, which cometh down out of*

heaven from my God: and I will write upon him my new name."

✟ Revelation 3:21:

"To him that overcometh will I grant to sit with me in my throne, even as I also overcame, and am set down with my Father in his throne."

I want to include one more, which could be called the ultimate promise of promises for the overcomer:

✟ Revelation 21:7:

"He that overcometh shall inherit all things; and I will be his God, and he shall be my son."

Could there ever be a better promise than that one? With all these promises for the overcomer in mind, let us proceed to the song, this great "anthem of the civil rights movement.

✞ Sing the song and let it change your life!

"We Shall Overcome" – Inspired by the Book of Revelation

We shall overcome, we shall overcome,

We shall overcome someday;

Oh, deep in my heart, I do believe,

We shall overcome someday.

The Lord will see us through, The Lord will

see us through,

The Lord will see us through someday;

Oh, deep in my heart, I do believe,

We shall overcome someday.

We're on to victory, We're on to victory,

We're on to victory someday;

Oh, deep in my heart, I do believe,

We're on to victory someday.

We'll walk hand in hand, we'll walk hand in

hand,

We'll walk hand in hand someday;

Oh, deep in my heart, I do believe,

We'll walk hand in hand someday.

We are not afraid, we are not afraid,

We are not afraid today;

Oh, deep in my heart, I do believe,

We are not afraid today.

The truth shall make us free, the truth shall

make us free,

The truth shall make us free someday;

Oh, deep in my heart, I do believe,

The truth shall make us free someday.

We shall live in peace, we shall live in

peace,

We shall live in peace someday;

Oh, deep in my heart, I do believe,

We shall live in peace someday.[36]

---

[36] We Shall Overcome, Anthem of the Civil Rights Movement

The Overcoming Testimony of the
Rev. Dr. Martin Luther King, Jr.

I cannot listen to or sing the song "We Shall Overcome" without thinking of the life and legacy of the Rev. Dr. Martin Luther King, Jr. The thing I love the most about Dr. King is that he boldly challenged racial hatred. His strength to love in the midst of hate brought him widespread respect as the prophet he truly was.

The Rev. Dr. Martin Luther King, Jr.'s sunrise was on January 15, 1929, and his sunset was on April 4, 1968. His grandfather began the family's long tenure as pastors of the now world-renowned Ebenezer Baptist Church in Atlanta, Georgia, serving from 1914 to 1931, succeeded by "Daddy" King, the Rev. Dr. Martin Luther King, Sr., who served until he died of a heart attack on November 11, 1984, at the age of 84. From 1960 until his death in 1968, the Rev. Dr. Martin Luther King, Jr. served as co-pastor.

I attended "Daddy" King's funeral on November 14, 1984, along with my father, the late Rev. Dr. Arthur L. Mackey, Sr., my mother, the Rev. Dr. Frances Mackey-Hull, and my cousin, Bishop J. Raymond Mackey. "Daddy" King was the man who prophesied that I would become the pastor of Mount Sinai Baptist Church.

From the beginning Martin Luther King, Jr. was an overcomer. After attending racially segregated public schools in Georgia, he graduated with extremely great honors from high school at the ripe young age of fifteen. He then proceeded to receive his B.A. degree in 1948 from the world-renowned Morehouse College, a distinguished Negro institution of learning in Atlanta, Georgia. Both his father, "Daddy" King, and his grandfather were graduates of Morehouse College as well. After three long years of intense theological training at Crozer Theological Seminary in Pennsylvania, where he was elected president of a predominantly white senior class, Martin, the young overcomer, was awarded his B.D. in 1951. After the training he received while at Crozer, he enrolled in graduate studies at Boston University, completing his residence for the doctorate in 1953 and obtaining his degree in 1955. While in

Boston, Martin met and married Coretta Scott, a highly regarded Christian young woman of great purpose, destiny, uncommon intellectual and artistic attainments. Four children were born out of the union of the Rev. Dr. and Mrs. King.

In 1954, Dr. King accepted the pastorate of the historic Dexter Avenue Baptist Church in Montgomery, Alabama. Always a strong soldier and hard worker for civil rights for members of his race, Dr. King was, by this time, a member of the executive committee of the National Association for the Advancement of Colored People (NAACP), the leading organization of its kind in the nation. He was ready, then, early in December 1955, to accept the visionary leadership of the first great Negro nonviolent demonstration of contemporary times in the United States, the Montgomery bus boycott described by Gunnar Jahn in his heart-moving presentation speech in honor of the Nobel Prize laureate. The boycott lasted a long 382 days. On December 21, 1956, after the United States Supreme Court had actually declared unconstitutional the laws requiring segregation on buses, Negroes and whites rode the buses as equals. During these difficult days of the Montgomery Bus Boycott, Dr. King , a brave overcomer, was arrested many times, his family's life was endangered, his very own home was viciously bombed by local racists, and he was literally subjected to personal abuse, but at the same time he clearly emerged as an overcomer, a Negro Christian leader of the first class rank, order, and file.

In 1957, Dr. King, was elected as the first president of the Southern Christian Leadership Conference (SCLC), an organization formed to provide dynamic new leadership for the now burgeoning civil rights movement. He took the ideals for this organization from the principles of Christianity, the principles of the Ultimate Overcomer, Jesus Christ, and its operational techniques from Mahatma Gandhi. In the eleven-year period between 1957 and 1968, Dr. King traveled over six million miles and spoke over twenty-five hundred times, appearing wherever there was injustice, protest, and action. Meanwhile, he wrote five books, as well as numerous articles.

The heart and soul of the overcomer was clearly exemplified through the social justice outreach ministry of Dr. King. In these years, he boldly and bravely led a massive protest in Birmingham, Alabama, that literally caught the attention of the entire world, providing what he called a "coalition of conscience" in his inspiring and historic "Letter from a

Birmingham Jail," a crystal clear manifesto of the Negro revolution. Following this, Dr. King planned the now historic voter's rights drives in Alabama, the seat of Satan for deep Southern racism, for the registration of Negroes as voters. He also directed the peaceful and also historic March on Washington, D.C., for Jobs and Freedom, of 250,000 people— overcomers of all races nationwide—to whom he delivered his classic address, "1 Have a Dream." He conferred with US President, John F. Kennedy and campaigned for his successor, President Lyndon B. Johnson. He was actually arrested while fighting for civil and human rights in racially segregated America upwards of twenty times and literally assaulted at least four times prior to his murder. He was awarded five honorary degrees, was named Man of the Year by *Time* magazine in 1963, and became not only the symbolic visionary leader of American blacks, but also a highly regarded world figure who spoke to the very heart and soul of the nations as a 20th-century prophet.

At the age of thirty-five, the Rev. Dr. King, a true overcomer, was the youngest man to have received the highly prestigious Nobel Peace Prize. When Dr. King was notified of his historic selection, he immediately announced that he would turn over the highly coveted prize money of $54,123 to the overall furtherance of the civil rights movement in racially segregated America. Dr. King gave his very life in service for others. King once said that "Everybody can be great, because everybody can serve. You don't have to have a college degree to serve. You don't have to make your subject and your verb agree to serve. You don't have to know about Plato and Aristotle to serve. You don't have to know Einstein's "Theory of Relativity" to serve. You don't have to know the Second Theory of Thermal Dynamics in Physics to serve. You only need a heart full of grace, a soul generated by love, and you can be that servant."[37]

On the evening of April 4, 1968, while standing on the balcony of his motel room in Memphis, Tennessee, while he was in town to lead a protest march in support of and sympathy with striking garbage workers of that city, the Rev. Dr. Martin Luther King Jr. was viciously assassinated. King was a Christian martyr as were the apostles of Christ. Like the

---

[37] Excerpted from "The Drum Major Instinct", a sermon by Rev. Martin Luther King, Jr., 1968. *A Knock At Midnight: Inspiration from the Great Sermons of Reverend Martin Luther King, Jr.*

Lutheran Pastor and theologian, Diertach Bonhoeffer of Germany whom Hilter lynched, King was only 39 years old. My father, Rev. Dr. Arthur L. Mackey, Sr. and Deacon Eddie Bryant attended the funeral of Dr. King, as Civil and Human Rights representatives from New York, and Times Square Department (TSS) in Hempstead, whom my father worked for, and Abraham & Straus Department Store (A & S), also in Hempstead at the time, paid their airfare and hotel in Atlanta, Georgia. Many years earlier in a speech in Detroit, Michigan, Dr. King stated: "If a man hasn't discovered something he will die for, he isn't fit to live."[38] They killed the dreamer, but the dream lives on and the spirit of the overcomer is still alive. The life of Dr. King taught us that the revelation of Jesus Christ, the Ultimate Overcomer, is still relevant to the issues of everyday life.

4) "Great Day"

✞ Revelation 6:16-17:

"And said to the mountains and rocks, Fall on us, and hide us from the face of him that sitteth on the throne, and from the wrath of the Lamb: For the great day of his wrath is come; and who shall be able to stand?"

---

[38] Rev. Dr. Martin Luther King, Jr., Speech in Detroit, Michigan, 1963

✝ **"Great Day" – Inspired by the Book of Revelation**

> Oh, the mourners will be runnin' on that great day
>
> (3 times)
>
> Cryin', who shall be able to stand?
>
> Lord, my mother will be restin' on that great day,
>
> who shall be able to stand?
>
> Oh, the deacons will be marchin' on that great day,
>
> who shall be able to stand?
>
> Oh, the sinners will be marchin' on that great day,
>
> who shall be able to stand?
>
> Oh, my Lord's gettin' us ready for that great day,
>
> who shall be able to stand?
>
> Oh, Jesus will be comin' on that great day, who
>
> shall be able to stand? [39]

5) "Listen To The Angels Shouting.

✝ **Revelation 7:1-3**

---

[39] GREAT DAY, Negro Spiritual

216

"And after these things I saw four angels standing on the four corners of the earth, holding the four winds of the earth, that the wind should not blow on the earth, nor on the sea, nor on any tree. And I saw another angel ascending from the east, having the seal of the living God: and he cried with a loud voice to the four angels, to whom it was given to hurt the earth and the sea, Saying, Hurt not the earth, neither the sea, nor the trees, till we have sealed the servants of our God in their foreheads."

✝ **Revelation 8:5-7:**

"And the angel took the censer, and filled it with fire of the altar, and cast it into the earth: and there were voices, and thunderings, and lightnings, and an earthquake. And the seven angels which had the seven trumpets prepared themselves to sound. The first angel sounded, and there followed hail and fire mingled with blood, and they were cast upon the earth: and the third part of trees was burnt up, and all green grass was burnt up."

✝ **"Listen to the Angels Shouting" – Inspired by the Book of Revelation**

Where do you think I found my soul, Listen to the angels shouting,

I found my soul at hell's dark door, Listen to the angels shouting,

Before I lay in hell one day, listen to the angels shouting,

I sing and pray my soul away, Listen to the angels shouting.

Run all the way, run all the way, run all the way my Lord,

Listen to the angels shouting

Blow, Gabriel, blow, Blow, Gabriel, Blow, Tell all the joyful news

Listen to the angels shouting,

I don't know what sinner want to stay here for.

Listen to the angels shouting,

When he gets home he will sorrow no more,

Listen to the angels shouting.

Brethren, will you come to the Promised Land,

Listen to the angels shouting,

Come all and sing within the heavenly land

Listen to the angels shouting.[40]

6) "Oh Freedom"

✟ Revelation 7:17:

"For the Lamb which is in the midst of the throne shall feed them, and shall lead them unto living fountains of waters: and God shall wipe away all tears from their eyes."

✟ Revelation 21:4:

"And God shall wipe away all tears from their eyes; and there shall be no more death, neither sorrow, nor crying, neither shall there be any more pain: for the former things are passed away."

✟ "Oh Freedom" – Inspired by the Book of Revelation

Oh Freedom! Oh freedom! Oh freedom over me

And before I'll be a slave I'll be buried in my grave

And go home to my Lord and be free.

No mo' moanin'

No mo' weepin'

There'll be singin'

---

[40] Listen To The Angels Shouting, Negro Spiritual

There'll be shoutin'

There'll be prayin'

And before I'll be a slave I'll be buried in my grave

And go home to my Lord and be free.[41]

7) "Walk in Jerusalem Just Like John"

✝ **Revelation 21:2, 10:**

"And I John saw the holy city, new Jerusalem, coming down from God out of heaven, prepared as a bride adorned for her husband....And he carried me away in the spirit to a great and high mountain, and showed me that great city, the holy Jerusalem, descending out of heaven from God."

✝ **"Walk in Jerusalem Just Like John" – Inspired by the Book of Revelation**

I want to be ready, I want to be ready, I want to be ready....

To walk in Jerusalem just like John.

---

41 Oh Freedom, Negro Spiritual

John said the city was just foursquare,

Walk in Jerusalem just like John.

And he declared he'd meet me there,

Walk in Jerusalem just like John.

Oh, John! Oh, John! What do you say?

Walk in Jerusalem just like John,

That I'll be there at the coming day,

Walk in Jerusalem just like John.

When Peter was preaching at Pentecost,

Walk in Jerusalem just like John,

He was endowed with the Holy Ghost

Walk in Jerusalem just like John. [42]

In his life changing sermon, "The Dimensions of a Complete Life", Rev. Dr. Martin Luther King, Jr. stated concerning the eternal truth that the revelation of Jesus written via John is relevant to everyday life from here to eternity. He said, "Thank God for John, who centuries ago caught a vision of the New Jerusalem. God grant that those of us who still walk the road of life will catch this vision and decide to move forward to that

---

[42] Walk In Jerusalem Just Like John, Negro Spiritual

city of complete life in which the length and the breadth and the height are equal." [43]

Seven Truths Concerning the New Jerusalem Found In Revelation 22

1. Revelation 22:1-2 teaches that the river of life is in the New Jerusalem.

2. Revelation 22:2 and 14 speak of the tree of life being in the Holy City.

3. Revelation 22:1-3 declares that the throne of God is in it.

4. Revelation 22:1-3 declares that the Lamb of God is in it.

5. Revelation 22:3 says that the New Jerusalem is a place with no curse of any kind.

6. Revelation 22:5 says that the Holy City operates totally off divine light, with no candle of natural sunlight, Jesus literally lights the New Jerusalem up

---

[43] Ibid, Martin Luther King Jr.

as He did during the first three days of creation prior to God making the sun on the fourth day.

7. Revelation 22:17 declares the classic threefold invitation to come to the New Jerusalem just like John: *"The Spirit and the bride say, Come. Let him that heareth say, Come. And Let him that is athirst Come. And whosoever will, let him take the water of life freely"*.

Seven Key Names for Jesus in Revelation Chapter 22

1. In Revelation 22:1-Jesus is called the Lamb.

2. In Revelation 22:5-6 and 20-21 Jesus is called Lord.

3. In Revelation 22:13 Jesus calls Himself the Alpha and the Omega.

4. In Revelation 22:13 Jesus calls Himself the First and the Last.

5. In Revelation 22:13 Jesus calls Himself the Beginning and the End.

6. In Revelation 22:16 Jesus calls Himself the Root and Offspring of David.

7. In Revelation 22:16 Jesus calls Himself the Bright and Morning Star.

Anybody who has ever grown up in church, or attended church just a little bit, or who has any clue at all as to what the Kingdom of God is all about should recognize that the seven names for Jesus found in Revelation 22 are the same exact classic names used for Jesus in the church. These are the seven main titles or names of Jesus that are used in our testimonies, songs, and sermons. Long before we knew what *Jehovah Jirah*, *El Shaddai*, and *Jehovah Nissi* even meant, long before we studied Hebrew and Greek Bible words, these were the basic names for Jesus. These names come straight out of Revelation 22. Revelation chapter 22 is the end of the New Testament, the end of the Book of Revelation, and the end of the Bible.

Notes For The Overcomer

CHAPTER SEVEN

Learning in Sevens: The Enduring Legacy of the Book of Revelation

God is looking for us to say, "Lord, I am available to you." My father, Rev. Arthur Mackey, Sr. was born as an incubator baby in Brooklyn, New York. At birth, he weighed two pounds, three ounces. His first bed was a dresser drawer. No one thought he would survive, but he was an overcomer.

From a very young age it became apparent that the call of God was upon his life. His father, the Rev. Walter R. Mackey, Sr., my grandfather, moved the family from Brooklyn to Long Island, where he founded Mt. Sinai Baptist Church Cathedral, where I now pastor. He literally built that church with his bare hands, and my father and his brothers and friends were all there supporting the work.

Rev. Dr. A. L. Mackey, Sr.

My father went to college at Virginia Union University, where I also attended. He met my mother there, and after they married, he came back to pastor in Roosevelt. My mother wanted to go to the jungles of Africa as a missionary, but my father said, "I'm going to bring you back to the jungles of Roosevelt, and you can be a missionary and first lady right there. The Lord tremendously blessed their ministry. He went on to become a great leader in human rights and civil rights within Nassau County, literally helping to stop riots within the community, and to help people get jobs and housing. On December 26, 1999, in an article appropriately entitled, "A Minister in Many Pulpits", the New York Times said of him: "Dr. Mackey met at the White House with Presidents Johnson, Reagan, Bush and Clinton. He had a one-on-one relationship with several Nassau County executives -- Thomas Gulotta,

Francis Purcell and Ralph Caso -- as well as Senator Alfonse D'Amato, his wife said. Nassau's Republican candidates often campaigned at his church. And he was a friend of Martin Luther King Sr., who preached at the Mount Sinai Baptist Church in 1980.

During the 1971 Hempstead riots, his daughter Vivian Mackey-Johnson recalled, the police asked his help in calming the community. He never failed to assist the drug users and the indigent who rang his doorbell seeking help. And every Christmas for more than 20 years, he cooked a giant vat of spaghetti and picked up bags of toys for the children of single parents in his congregation."[44] My father did a tremendous work for the Lord because of his availability to God.

That's all it takes. Let God know, "Lord, I am available to you. Here I am Lord, send me. Everything I am, everything I'm not, everything I have, and everything I've got, here I am, send me." It is also important to say, "Here I am, Lord, teach me." Teaching eternal truths in sets of seven is the enduring teaching

---

[44] The New York Times, Lives Lived Well And the Lessons That They Teach, A MINISTER IN MANY PULPITS, December 26, 1999

style established by Jesus Christ Himself, as is evident particularly in the Book of Revelation. This extremely effective teaching method established by Jesus works well with other Bible lessons as well.

The Touch of Jesus - Empowered to Minister

✝ **Matthew 8:14-15**

"And when Jesus was come into Peter's house, he saw his wife's mother laid, and sick of a fever. And he touched her hand, and the fever left her: and she arose, and ministered unto them."

1. The Entrance of Jesus: *"And when Jesus was come into Peter's house..."*

2. The Eyesight of Jesus: *"...he saw his wife's mother..."*

3. The Insight of Jesus: *"...laid, and sick of a fever..."*

4. The Involvement of Jesus: *"...and he touched her hand..."*

5. The Effectiveness of Jesus: *"...and the fever left her..."*

6. The Impact of Jesus: *"...and she arose..."*

7. The Empowering Influence of Jesus: *"...and*

ministered unto them."

Seven Things God Says Are Ready

There are seven things God says are ready.

1. The sinner is ready to perish (Deuteronomy 26:3).

2. God is ready to pardon (Nehemiah 9:17).

3. The Lord is ready to save (Isaiah 38:20).

4. The saint is ready to every good work (Titus 3:1).

5. The servant is ready to preach (Romans 1:15).

6. The glory is ready to be revealed (1 Peter 1:5).

7. The Lord is ready to judge (1 Peter 4:5)

These are seven things God says are ready throughout His Word. His Word lets us know that He is ready. Are we ready to say, yes, to the Lord and show our availability to Him?

Seven Right Links In The Chain of God's Grace

Second Corinthians 5:1-20 brings out seven right "links" in the chain of God's grace:

1. The first link is the new nature, the new creation in Christ (2 Corinthians 5:17).

2. The second link is the new standing in Christ (2 Corinthians 5:17).

3. The third link is the new life, not self, but Christ (2 Corinthians 5:15).

4. The fourth link is the new motive, love of Christ (2 Corinthians 5:14).

5. The fifth link is the new path, not by sight but by faith (2 Corinthians 5:7).

6. The sixth link is new service, being an ambassador for Christ

    (2 Corinthians 5:20).

7. The seventh link in the chain of God's grace is the new home, Heaven, (2 Corinthians 5:1).

Seven Stars In the Scripture

Scripture gives seven specific references to stars:

1. The general star of prophecy that points us to Christ (Numbers 24:17).

2. The guiding star of Bethlehem that leads us to Christ (Matthew 2:2).

3. The gracious star of ministry that guides us to Christ (Revelation 1:20).

4. The gleaming stars of light that remind us of Christ (Jeremiah 31:35).

5. The gathering stars of hope that draw us to Christ (Revelation 22:16; 2 Peter 1:19).

6. The glory stars of Heaven that shine like Christ (1 Corinthians 15:41-42; Daniel 12:8).

7. The great stars of warning that usher in Christ (Luke 21: 25-26).

Helen Keller once said, "I am only one, but still I am one; I cannot do everything, but still I can do something. I will not refuse to do the something I can do." Like Helen Keller, we need to learn to do the best we can while we can. We cannot do everything, but we can do something to make a difference.

Wisdom's Seven Cries To The World

God's wisdom has seven cries to the world that we live in:

1. The cry for starving sinners to come for the bread of life.

2. The cry for ignorant sinners to come for the wisdom of God.

3. The cry for wandering sinners, to come to the house of God.

4. The cry for needy sinners to come to the power of God.

5. The cry for empty sinners, to come to the fullness of God.

6. The cry for ruined sinners to come to the redemption of God.

7. The cry for seeking sinners to come to the welcome of God.

Seven Promises of the Rain of the Spirit in Joel Chapter 2

✝ **Joel 2:23-29**

"Be glad then, ye children of Zion, and rejoice in the LORD your God: for he hath given you the former rain moderately, and he will cause to come down for you the rain, the former rain, and the latter rain in the first month. And the floors shall be full of wheat, and the vats shall overflow with wine and oil. And I will restore to you the years that the locust

hath eaten, the cankerworm, and the caterpillar, and the palmerworm, my great army which I sent among you. And ye shall eat in plenty, and be satisfied, and praise the name of the LORD your God, that hath dealt wondrously with you: and my people shall never be ashamed. And ye shall know that I am in the midst of Israel, and that I am the LORD your God, and none else: and my people shall never be ashamed. And it shall come to pass afterward, that I will pour out my spirit upon all flesh; and your sons and your daughters shall prophesy, your old men shall dream dreams, your young men shall see visions: And also upon the servants and upon the handmaids in those days will I pour out my spirit. "

These verses reveal seven promises regarding the rain of the Holy Spirit:

1. The Former and the Latter Rain—A Double Portion (Joel 2:23)
2. Fullness and Overflow—Supernatural Provision (Joel 2:24)
3. Devine Restoration (Joel 2:25)
4. Wondrous Dealings of God (Joel 2:26)

5. Divine Awareness of God's Presence (Joel 2:27)

6. Outpouring of the Spirit on Sons and Daughters, Old and Young (Joel 2:28)

7. Outpouring of the Spirit on Servants and Handmaidens (the economically oppressed; Joel 2:29)

Seven Aspects of Love

The Scriptures raise up seven aspects of love, not just in the typical love verses that we hear about and talk about so often, but also in some verses that are not as familiar, such as:

1. John 15:9, dealing with the infinite aspect of love.

2. Jeremiah 31:3, dealing with the everlasting aspect of love.

3. Galatians 2:20, dealing with the perfect aspect of love.

4. Romans 5:8, dealing with the commended aspect of love.

5. John 23:3, dealing with the unchanging aspect of love.

6. Romans 8:35, dealing with the inseparable aspect of love.

7. Second Corinthians 5:14, dealing with the constraining aspect of love.

As Christian believers, we also have a seven-fold responsibility related to love. As we deal with *Seven Levels of Promise for the Overcomer*, we also need to look at our seven-fold responsibility. This is outlined clearly in the Word as we meditate, not just on one scripture, but look at the whole counsel of God:

1. Our responsibility to love all men (1 Thessalonians 3:12).
2. Our responsibility to be patient to all men (1 Thessalonians 5:14).
3. Our responsibility to live peaceably with all men (Romans 12:18).
4. Our responsibility to provide all things in the sight of all (Romans 7:17).
5. Our responsibility to be gentle to all men (2 Timothy 2:24).
6. Our responsibility to let our moderation be known to all (Philippians 4:5).
7. Our responsibility to do good unto all men (Galatians 6:10).

As Christian believers, we cannot get away from our responsibility in the basic things that the Word of God talks about. We have to embrace our complete, seven-fold responsibility that arises out of timeless teachings of Scripture.

Seven Eternal Things Clearly Taught in Scripture

Scripture clearly teaches many things, not least of which is the fact that there are seven eternal things:

1. The eternal God, the source of all (Deuteronomy . 33:27).
2. Eternal redemption, the cause of all (Hebrews 9:12).
3. Eternal salvation, God's greatest work (Hebrews 5:9).
4. Eternal life, God's richest gift (Romans 4:23).
5. Eternal inheritance as the saint's possession (Hebrews 9:15).
6. Eternal glory, the believer's hope (1 Peter 5:10).
7. Eternal fire, the sinner's doom (Jude 7).

These seven eternal things help us realize even more that the revelation is relevant and that there is substance to what God is saying to us. His is not a fly by night message, but one with which He wants to bring us to our knees in repentance and to get our focus back on, *"Not my will be done, but Thy will be done."*

Seven Things That God Never Does

God can do anything, but there are seven things that God *never* does:

1. God never breaks His covenant. Judges 2:1 lets us know that, *"God never suffers the righteous to be moved."*

2. Second Timothy 2:19 reiterates the same truth.

3. God never leaves us or forsakes us (Hebrews 13:5).

4. God never allows evil to overcome good (Proverbs 10:30; Romans 8:37). Although from our limited perspective it seems sometimes that evil has the upper hand, ultimately evil will be destroyed. This is as certain in God's sovereign will as though it had already happened.

5. God never lets His children, His overcomers, be ashamed (2 Timothy1: 12).

6. God never allows His children to perish. If we are in Christ, we will not perish, but have everlasting life (John 3:16; 10:28; Jude 24-25).

7. God will never allow His kingdom to be destroyed. God's kingdom is eternal (Daniel 2:44; Hebrews 7:28).

Seven Dimensions of Christian Fellowship

There are also seven dimensions of Christian fellowship revealed in the Word of God. These, too, are important to our overall understanding of the *Seven Levels of Promise for the Overcomer*, because they will arm us with vital information for your everyday Christian walk, and with ammunition for fighting and conquering the enemy. So what are the seven dimensions of Christian fellowship?

1. Fellowship with the Father (Acts 2:42).
2. The fellowship of Christ (1 Corinthians 1:9).
3. The fellowship of communion (1 John 1:3).
4. The fellowship of love (Galatians 2:9).
5. The fellowship of suffering (Philippians 3:10).
6. The fellowship of the Spirit (Philippians 2:1).
7. The fellowship of service (Philippians 1:5).

Seven Ways of the Overcomer

Jesus is the way, the truth, and the life, but He is also the Ultimate Overcomer. In Colossians 1:9-12, we can find seven ways, attitudes or behaviors that will help us persevere because they follow the example of Jesus.

✝ Colossians 1:9-12:

"For this cause we also, since the day we heard it, do not cease to pray for you, and to desire that ye might be filled with the knowledge of his will in all wisdom and spiritual understanding; That ye might walk worthy of the Lord unto all pleasing, being fruitful in every good work, and increasing in the knowledge of God; Strengthened with all might, according to his glorious power, unto all patience and longsuffering with joyfulness; Giving thanks unto the Father, which hath made us meet to be partakers of the inheritance of the saints in light."

Here, then, are the seven ways of the overcomer:

1. Knowledge: knowing the will of God.

2. Walking: walking in the way of God.

3. Work: working the work of God.

4. Waiting: waiting for the time of God.

5. Suffering: suffering patiently for God.

6. Rejoicing: rejoicing in God.

7. Thankfulness: being thankful to God.

Seven Points that We Learn through Baptism

A young man in our church recently accepted Jesus as his personal Lord and Savior. After he gave his life to Christ, he came forward and said that he wanted to be baptized, so we prepared him for baptism. There are seven aspects of baptism that all who have received Jesus as Lord and Savior need to understand. As believers, we want to let the world know that we are living for God. It is not physical water baptism in the water that saves us. Water baptism is a godly symbol of what happened in our heart during our conversion experience. The thief on the cross did not have a chance to be baptized, yet when he expressed his faith in Christ, he received the promise that he would be with the Lord in paradise that very day.

Baptism symbolizes the new life we have in Jesus. As we stand up in the water of the baptistery, we symbolize the life of Christ. Our immersion into the water symbolizes His death, as well as the death of our old life and nature of sin: *"buried with Him by baptism into death."* Our rising up from the water symbolizes Jesus' resurrection, and how we have been *"raised to walk in newness of life."* But what else does the Bible teach us about baptism?

1. Baptism is a divine command to be obeyed (Matthew 28:19; Mark 16:16).

2. Baptism is a sign of conversion to be experienced. It is not conversion, but a sign of conversion, which is a very important distinction (Acts 2:42).

3. Baptism is a confession of faith to be intelligent. When we make this confession of faith it is very meaningful, and people want to come and witness our baptism (Acts 8:36-38).

4. Baptism is a testimony of Christ to the public. When we are baptized, we are making a public statement

declaring our conversion and change of life (Acts 10:48; 16:30-34).

5. Baptism is a picture of spiritual experience to be known (Romans 6:4). Therefore, it also speaks of things to come in our growth and in our relationship with our Lord and Savior Jesus Christ.

6. Baptism is a mark of separation to be accepted (Colossians 2:12). It makes a line of demarcation, a line of separation that says we are living for the Lord, and so are living distinct from the world. It is our message to the world that we have accepted the salvation God has offered through His Son.

7. Baptism is a figure of the resurrected life to be lived (1 Peter 3:21). Baptism points to the resurrection of Jesus Christ. The resurrected life that baptism represents is a life that is to be walked out and lived out everyday.

The Seven Songs of the Saved

The Scriptures highlight seven songs of the saved. There are many songs in the Bible, but these seven really stand out, and have been recognized across two millennia of church history as particularly significant.

1. The new song, the song of life, as exemplified primarily in the Psalms.

2. The Lord's song, the song of praise.

3. The home song, the song of joy.

4. The salvation song, the song of gratitude (Psalm 32:7).

5. The spiritual song, the song of fellowship (Ephesians 5:19).

6. The pilgrim song, the song of gladness (Isaiah 35:10).

7. The redemption song, the song of glory (Revelation 15:3).

Seven Aspects of Preaching the Glorious Gospel of Jesus Christ

There are even seven aspects of preaching the glorious gospel of Jesus Christ, The Ultimate Overcomer, particularly as found in the eighth chapter of the Book of Acts.

1. The preaching of the Word (Acts 8:4).

2. The preaching of Christ (Acts 8:5).

3. The preaching of the kingdom (Acts 8:12).

4. The preaching of the Word of the Lord (Acts 8:25).

5. The preaching of the gospel (Acts 8:25).

6. The preaching of Jesus (Acts 8:35).

7. The preaching of the gospel *everywhere*, (Acts 8:40).

Seven Things that we do by Faith

Now there are also seven things that we do by faith, as we talk about "Seven Levels of Promise for the Overcome." We really need to get these seven things deep into our spirit.

1. We live by faith (Galatians 2:20).

2. We stand by faith (2 Corinthians 1:24).

3. We walk by faith (1 Corinthians 5:7).

4. We endure by faith (Romans 11:27).

5. We subdue by faith (Hebrews 11:33).

6. We fight by faith (1 Timothy 6:12).

7. We overcome by faith (1 John 5:4).

Seven-fold Privilege of Being a Child of God

Being saved—being a child of God—brings a seven-fold privilege to every believer.

1. Saved (Deuteronomy 33:29).

2. Secured (Deuteronomy 33:3).

3. Separated (Deuteronomy 33:16).

4. Satisfied (Deuteronomy 33:23).

5. Sheltered (Deuteronomy 33:29).

6. Seated (Deuteronomy 33:3).

7. Sacrificing (Deuteronomy 33:19).

Seven Dimensions of the Christian Life

The Christian life has seven important dimensions, each of which is a vital part of becoming an overcomer.

1. Confession of Christ (John 12:42).

2. Cleansing by Christ (John 13:10).

3. Communion with Christ (John 13:23).

4. Chastening unto Christ (John 15:2).

5. Comfort in Christ (John 16:33).

6. Consecrated to Christ (John 15:14).

7. Conflict for Christ (John 15:19).

Seven Things that are Set

In the Scriptures we learn that there are seven things that are set, seven things that are definite, beyond a shadow of doubt.

1. A set child (Luke 2:34).

2. A set light (Acts 13:47).

3. A set ruler (Hebrews 2:7).

4. A set hope (Hebrews 6:18).

5. A set priest (Hebrews 8:1).

6. A set race (Hebrews 12:1).

7. A set joy (Hebrews 12:2).

Seven Pure Things

The world is filled with impure things. Thank God that there are seven pure things revealed in Scripture upon which we can focus our minds.

1. Pure wisdom (James 3:17).

2. Pure water (Hebrews 10:22).

3. Pure mind (2 Peter 3:1).

4. Pure heart (1 Peter 1:22).

5. Pure conscience (1 Timothy 3:9).

6. Pure religion (James 1:27).

7. Pure servant (1 Timothy 5:22).

Seven "I Wills" of the Great Jehovah

Exodus chapter 6 tells us that there are seven "I wills" of God Almighty.

1. *"I will bring you,"* (verse 6).
2. *"I will rid you,"* (verse 6).
3. *"I will redeem you,"* (verse 6).
4. *"I will take you,"* (verse 7).
5. *"I will be to you,"* (verse 7).
6. *"I will bring you,"* (verse 8).
7. *"I will give to you,"* (verse 8).

Seven Things To Flee From

Scripture also reveals seven things from which we are to flee as children of God.

1. Flee the wrath to come (Matthew 3:7).
2. Flee fornication (1 Corinthians 6:8).
3. Flee idolatry (1 Corinthians10:14).
4. Flee youthful lust (1 Timothy 2:22).
5. Flee strangers that would bring us into ungodliness (John 10:5).
6. Flee mammon (1 Timothy 6:11).

7. Flee persecution (Matthew 10:23).

Seven Things to Continue In

In contrast to things we should flee, there are seven things we should to continue in, seven things we should embrace as believers.

1. Continue in God's Word (John 8:31).
2. Continue in God's love (John 15:9).
3. Continue in God's grace (Acts 13:42).
4. Continue in the faith (Acts 14:22).
5. Continue in prayer (Colossians 4:2).
6. Continue in brotherly love (Hebrews 13:1).
7. Continue in following the Lord (1 Samuel 12:14).

Seven Main Scriptures
that Teach Us Not to be Slothful

There are seven main Scriptures that teach us not to be slothful.

1. Work out your own salvation with fear and trembling (Philippians 2:12).
2. Fight the good fight of faith (1 Timothy 6:12).
3. Grow in grace (2 Peter 3:18).

4. Be instant in season and out of season (2 Timothy 4:2).

5. Study to show yourself approved (2 Timothy 2:5).

6. Earnestly contend for the faith (Jude 3).

7. Be not slothful, but be fervent in spirit, serving the Lord (Romans 12:11).

The Seven Abundant Things

As we talk about *Seven Levels of Promise for the Overcomer*, God has seven abundant things that have content, things that have meaning, things that can help pull us through any trial, tribulation, or calamity.

1. Abundant mercy (1 Peter 1:3); abundant mercy for the lost.

2. Abundant grace (1 Peter 1:14); abundant grace for the needy.

3. Abundant pardon (the entire Book of Isaiah); abundant pardon for the guilty.

4. Abundant life (John 10:10); abundant life for the dead.

5. Abundant power (Ephesians 3:20); abundant power for the weak.

6. Abundant peace (Psalm 37:11); abundant peace for the troubled.

7. Abundant joy (Philippians 1:26); abundant joy for the sad.

In his outstanding book entitled *Becoming A Stretcher Bearer* noted author Michael Slater gives a list of seven outstanding gifts that Jesus, the ultimate Overcomer utilized in His public ministry.

1. Teaching

2. Encouragement and support

3. Healing

4. Prophecy

5. Faith

6. Discernment

7. Evangelism

Out of this list of seven, Mr. Slater states that: "Jesus' most outstanding gift: *the gift of encouragement and support.*"[45] God

---

[45] Michael Slater, Becoming A Stretcher Bearer – Lifting One Another in Times of Need with the Gifts of Encouragement and Support, Regal Books, Ventura, California, 1985, 1989, pg 46

pulls off the covers and shows us things that are relevant for what we are going through today, just as He did for John and his contemporaries two millennia ago. If John could be faithful and fruitful, then we can be faithful and fruitful for God also. It is not easy but it can be done, because in Jesus we are equipped to be overcomers.

Notes For The Overcomer

CHAPTER EIGHT

Called to Be an Overcomer

A t this point in our discussion of *Seven Levels of Promise for the Overcomer*, it would be helpful to take a closer look at the word "overcome," particularly as found in the writings of St. John. Of course, our main biblical text for this book is the Book of Revelation, which John received from Jesus Christ toward the end of his life. But even as far back as John 16:33, Jesus says, *"These things I have spoken unto you, that in me ye might have peace. In the world you shall have tribulation: but be of good cheer; I have overcome the world."* From this we can see that the message of *Seven Levels of Promise for the Overcomer* was established at the very beginning of Christ's ministry. It is inevitable that in the world we are going to have tribulation, pressures, and problems. We will experience all types of challenging situations, but Jesus said, *"Be of good cheer."* Why? Because

He has overcome the world, and we overcome also because we are in Him.

Overcoming the Wicked One

This concept of the overcomer is presented very clearly in John's first epistle. For example, First John 2:13 says, *"I write unto you, fathers, because ye have known Him that is from the beginning. I write unto you, young men, because ye have overcome the wicked one. I write unto you little children, because ye have known the Father."* John writes to a "trinity" of the fathers, the young men, and the little children. He says to the young men that they have overcome the wicked one. There is an enemy out there who must be confronted.

Continuing on, John says in the next verse, *"I have written unto you fathers, because ye have known Him that is from the beginning. I have written unto you young men, because you are strong and the Word of God abideth in you and ye have overcome the wicked one"* (1 John 2:14). The fathers that he is writing to used to be young men. So when he says *"You have overcome the wicked one,"* he means that they have been in situations where they have overcome the wicked one, but even the young ones learn from the fathers how to overcome the wicked one, and because of that, they have overcome the wicked one. The wicked one is in the world today, and we have to learn how to overcome.

Hank Aaron, A True Overcomer

> Hank Aaron was and is a true overcomer. The true Spirit of God within Mr. Aaron was far greater than the deeply racist and negative spirit in the world that so forcibly opposed him.

World-renowned baseball player Henry Louis Aaron was born on February 5, 1934, in Mobile, Alabama. He grew up clearly understanding the evil reality of segregation in the Deep South and racism.

Aaron was and is a true overcomer who was, until recently, baseball's all-time home-run king. Hank Aaron played for 23 years as an outfielder for the Milwaukee (later Atlanta) Braves and the Milwaukee Brewers (1954 -76). Hank Aaron holds many of baseball's most distinguished records, including: runs batted in—2,297; extra base hits—1,477; total bases—6,856;

and most years with 30 or more home runs—15. Hank Aaron, a true overcomer, is also proudly numbered in the top five for all-time career hits and runs. In addition, Hank Aaron held the all-time record for the most career home runs – 755—until Barry Bonds broke it with his 756th home run on August 7, 2007 in San Francisco.

Breaking Babe Ruth's record of 714 career home runs was both a tremendous triumph and a constant trial for this true overcomer. Mr. Aaron was overwhelmed by the print, television, and radio media coverage he received, but at the same time, he was crucified in print, and threatened by deeply racist personalities who hated him for breaking Babe Ruth's record.

A wonderful all round player whose awesome skills were never fully appreciated until he broke the Babe's record in 1974, Hank Aaron was voted the National League's Most Valuable Player only once, in the year 1957.

After retiring as a highly accomplished player, Hank Aaron moved into the Atlanta Braves front office as executive vice-president, another historic accomplishment in Black History, where he was a leading representative for minority hiring in baseball. Hank Aaron, was finally elected to baseball's historic Hall of Fame in 1982.

Mr. Aaron's long-awaited and highly-anticipated autobiography entitled, *I Had a Hammer*, was published in the year 1990. In 1999, to celebrate Mr. Aaron's now historic 25th anniversary of breaking Babe Ruth's home run record, Major League Baseball officially announced the prestigious Hank Aaron Award, which is given every year to the very best overall hitter in each league.

Hank Aaron was honored with the prestigious Presidential Medal of Freedom in 2002. Hank Aaron was and is a true overcomer. The true Spirit of God within Mr. Aaron was far greater than the deeply racist and negative spirit in the world that so forcibly opposed him.

The Greater One Is Within Me

The most well-known Scripture by far is John 3:16, but 1 John 4:4 is not far behind: *"Ye are of God, little children, and have overcome them: because greater is he that is in you than he that is in the world."* So we have the assurance that the greater One is inside of us. The Spirit of God is inside of us, the

Spirit of the conquering King, the Spirit of the risen Savior. He who is in us is greater than He who is in the world. This means that whatever pressure is going on in our world, if we truly are living for God, if we truly have submitted our lives to God, we have the greater One, we have the Spirit of the Creator of the universe inside us to enable us to overcome any problem, any obstacle that can come our way.

No wonder, then, that during the Civil Rights Movement many sang a song with the words, "Deep in my heart I do believe that we shall overcome some day." They knew that God was inside of them, and if God was inside of them, they could overcome any obstacle that came their way. We need that same overcoming power in our world today; we need it in our churches today. That is the way we can overcome the spirit of the world: having the Spirit of Christ inside us.

The Believer in Jesus, the Son of God, Overcomes the World

First John 5:5 says, *"Who is he that overcometh the world, but he that believeth Jesus is the Son of God?"* Now we see the correlation of the themes. The Gospel of John mentions seven witnesses to Jesus as the Son of God: John the Baptist,

Nathaniel, Peter, the blind man that Jesus healed, Martha, John the apostle and Jesus Christ Himself.

The first epistle of John picks up again on this theme, and it is tied in to the theme of overcoming, so that all these things are central. In other words, this is a fresh word from God, this is *rhema*. *"Who is He that overcometh the world, but he that believeth Jesus is the Son of God."* In other words, you are not going to be an overcomer if you do not believe Jesus is the Son of God. If you really want to tap into the fullness of these principles, you have to realize that Jesus is the Son of the living God, and He has come to make a difference in your life.

In the New Testament Greek the word used for overcometh and overcome in First John and Book of Revelation is *nikao*. It means to conquer, prevail, get the victory. Christ being victorious over all His satanic foes, such as, death, hell, and the grave is a classic example of *nikao* in action. Christians that hold fast to their faith even unto death against the power of our daily foes, temptations, and persecutions is another example of *nikao* in action. This particular definition reminds me of one of my favorite songs sung by the living gospel legend, Deacon Eddie Bryant of the Mount Sinai Baptist Church Cathedral

Male Chorus. In the gospel song entitled "Hold On", Deacon Bryant sings the timeless words "Don't give up when things get rough / Just hold on / Hold on."

Remember the words to overcomers that Jesus gave to the seven churches of Asia Minor. Specifically, let's recall Revelation 2:7: *"To him that overcometh will I give to eat of the tree of life, which is in the midst of the paradise of God."* This is the promise that enabled the thief on the cross to become an overcomer, even at the time of his death, and to enter into paradise with Jesus.

Remember also Revelation 2:11: *"He that overcometh shall not be hurt of the second death."* The Bible says that it is appointed to man once to die and then the judgment. But when those who have been born again in Christ die and stand before the Lord in eternity, they will not have to worry about going through another death, the second death, eternal separation from God. The second death is only for those who die without repentance. All those who die in the Lord go before the judgment seat of Christ, *the Bema seat*, to determine rewards; eternal life is already assured. Those who die outside the safety of Christ, however, end up standing in the great white throne judgment. We know that God is everywhere, but the separation from God in terms of that closeness of relationship and intimacy with Him is what I am referring to.

This essential separation from God is the second death, and *no one* who truly is rooted and grounded in Christ will experience it. Revelation chapter 2:17 says: *"To him that overcometh will I give to eat of the hidden manna, and will give him a white stone, and in the stone a new name written, which no man knoweth saving he that receiveth it."* God has a name written that nobody else knows. Jesus is able to give us of the hidden manna; He is the Bread of Life.

Truly, we serve an awesome God. Revelation 2:26, says: *"He that overcometh, and keepeth my works until the end, to him will I give power over the nations."* If we keep His works until the end, if we keep His commandments until the end, He gives us power over the nations. We will be able to relate to, speak into, the life of any creed and any culture, because the gospel of Christ transcends all races, cultures, and creeds.

Revelation 3:5 says: *"He that overcometh, the same shall be clothed in white raiment; and I will not blot out his name out of the book of life, but I will confess his name before My Father, and before His angels."* Therefore, if we stay with God, our name is not going to be blotted out of the book of life. He is going to confess our name before the Father, and before all the angels, and declare us to be overcomers, just like Jesus Christ, our Lord.

Recall the promise of Revelation 3:12: *"Him that overcometh will I make a pillar in the temple of my God, and he shall go no more out: and I will write upon him the name of My God, and the name of the city of My God, which is new Jerusalem, which cometh down out of heaven, and I will write upon him my new name."* This overcoming theme is central throughout the Scriptures. In the New Testament, it is prominent, particularly in the writings of John: his Gospel, his three epistles, and the Book of Revelation.

Tony Dungy

The First African-American Coach to Win a Super Bowl

Coach Tony Dungy is a true Christian overcomer, whose success has not corrupted his soul.

Tony Dungy, a totally committed Christian, is the only National Football League player since the merger, ever to intercept a football pass and throw a football pass interception in the very same football game. Tony Dungy was the emergency quarterback for the Pittsburgh Steelers in an October 30, 1977 game against the Baltimore Colts, when both Terry Bradshaw and Mike Kruczek went down with injuries. Tony Dungy effectively played safety on defense in that memorable game. Tony Dungy is the very first National Football League head coach to defeat every single one of the 32 National Football League teams. At the age of 24, Tony Dungy was also the youngest assistant coach in the entire history of the National

Football League. Tony Dungy made the National Football League playoff as a head coach a total of nine times. Indianapolis Colts Coach, Tony Dungy and Chicago Bears Coach, Lovie Smith are the first African-Americans to coach a Super Bowl. On that historic day, February 3, 2007, Coach Dungy was the first African-American coach to win a Super Bowl. Coach Tony Dungy is a true Christian overcomer, whose success has not corrupted his soul.

The Faithful Witness – Helping The Innocent Overcome

Revelation 1:5

"And from Jesus Christ, who is the faithful witness, and the first begotten of the dead, and the prince of the kings of the earth. Unto him that loved us, and washed us from our sins in his own blood."

Faith Mackey

After preaching a Sunday morning message at the 11:00 a.m. service at Mount Sinai Baptist Church Cathedral in Roosevelt, New York, where I serve as Senior Pastor, my youngest daughter, Faith, came forward after the invitation for salvation. Since she was already saved she joined the church as a candidate for baptism. The following week, as my wife, Brenda, was walking Faith back to school after a brief mother-daughter lunch break, a vicious pit bull jumped out at Brenda and barked at her. When Faith saw the dog, she ran, and the pit bull went for her. She fell to the ground and the vicious pit bull went for Faith's head. Thank God, Faith listened to my wife, and put her hood over her head. The vicious pit bull had the hood in his mouth and was growling and griping on it with tremendous force. Brenda picked Faith up and yanked the hood out the pit bull's mouth. Brenda was now holding Faith in her arms and the dog was trying to jump up and get Faith. At that point the only thing that Brenda could do was yell "the blood of Jesus" and then she yelled for help. Two vans instantly drove up on the street that was empty seconds ago. One good neighbor said jump in the van, and the other good neighbor chased the dog back to its house. When I heard the story, I was furious. Our other two children, Yolanda and Jordan, were deeply concerned. Yet we had to stop and thank God for saving Brenda and Faith's life.

Through this incident, God revealed to me that when the enemy comes to attack our faith in God, he leaps for the head—the area of thoughts, choices, and decisions of life. John 10:10 states that: *"the thief cometh not, but for to steal, and to kill, and to destroy: I am come that they might have life, and that they might have it more abundantly."*

When I stood in the baptismal pool and saw Faith come down to be baptized, I had to thank God, because she was a little overcomer. The enemy desired to destroy her, but the blood of Jesus, the faithful witness, spared her from the vicious dog that tried to destroy her. Brenda and Faith went through a horrible situation, but thank God they came out alive. If Brenda would have let Faith walk to school alone she would have not survived. She was a faithful witness. The two good neighbors who helped Brenda and Faith were faithful witnesses.

Seven Scriptural Messages that Back Up

Seven Levels of Promise for the Overcomer

I want to discuss briefly seven scriptures that have inspired me with regard to this whole message of *Seven Levels of Promise for the Overcomer.* Each of these Scriptures really gets to the heart of the matter.

1.)   Jacob Works Seven More Years for His True Love
✝ **Genesis 29:20:**
"And Jacob served seven years for Rachel, and they seemed unto him but a few days, for the love he had to her."

Jacob had fallen in love with his uncle Laban's daughter, Rachel, and worked for his uncle for seven years to win her hand in marriage. But on the night of his marriage, his honeymoon night, he was tricked by Laban, who gave him his older daughter, Leah, instead. She was not the one who he was in love with. Jacob confronted Laban, after realizing he was tricked, and he arranged a deal to work seven more years to get Rachel as his wife. Now that is true love. Jacob was a trickster and now he had been tricked by another who was just as cunning. But Jacob was more than this. He was the one through whom God's promise to Abraham to build a great nation from his descendants would be fulfilled. Those seven extra years that Jacob worked to get Rachel truly represent the message of "Seven Levels of Promise for the Overcomer."

## 2.)	Seven Years of Plenty & Seven Years of Famine

Genesis chapter forty-one tells of Pharaoh's troubling dream in which seven fat and healthy cows were eaten by seven scrawny and sickly cows, and where seven healthy sheaves of grain were devoured by seven sickly sheaves. Joseph, a slave and prison inmate at the time, interpreted Pharaoh's dream as a prophecy from God of seven years of plenty followed by seven years of famine. Pharaoh promoted Joseph on the spot and made him prime minister, placing him in charge of planning and preparing for the coming years of plenty and famine.

The message of *Seven Levels of Promise for the Overcomer* is key in the Book of Genesis. In the forty-first chapter the number seven is mentioned very prominently, but even more important is the principle behind it. We need to use that principle to save in the seven years of prosperity, or periods of prosperity. The periods where there seems to be perfection—it may not even be seven years, it could be a longer or shorter time, but in those times of prosperity we need to save. We need to lay aside so that when the time of famine comes we will be well prepared.

I once went with my wife, Brenda, to the home of a young lady to pray for her. She had lost several children during pregnancy, and the Lord had finally blessed her and her husband with a child. During those previous years of heartache and disappointment, she had experienced job losses and great losses of wealth and income. Nevertheless, she began to save and invest. She stored up on canned food, and on different items that people normally would not think about. She laid money aside from her own personal business. After losing many children, the Lord blessed her and she miraculously became pregnant again. She had enough food and canned food stored up to take care of herself for a long period. She was not working, and had enough money in the bank in order to survive until she and her husband could get back to work. She was using this principle of *Seven Levels of Promise for the Overcomer* that we see clearly throughout the Scriptures. In

Joseph's case, he rose from being sold into slavery by his jealous brothers, to being placed in charge of his master's household and assets. Then he was falsely accused of raping his master's wife, and ended up in prison. From prison, he interpreted the dreams of the butler and the baker which opened the door two years later for him to be brought before Pharaoh to interpret the king's dream. Pharaoh recognized Joseph's exceptional character and quality, and made him second in command.

Joseph directed the storage and laying up of food from the seven years of prosperity against the seven years of famine. When the time of famine arrived, Joseph's brothers came to Egypt looking for food. They ended up kneeling before Joseph, whom they did not recognize. The brother they had hatefully thrown into a pit and sold into slavery, now ruled as second-in-command in Egypt. God turned everything around, allowing the one who seemed to be a victim to become the victor, and to experience these levels of promise for the overcomer.

3.)   Seven Things The Lord Does Not Like
   ✝ **Proverbs 6:16-19:**

"These six things doth the LORD hate: yea, seven are an abomination unto him: A proud look, a lying tongue, and hands that shed innocent blood, An heart that deviseth wicked imaginations, feet that be swift in running to mischief, A false witness that speaketh lies, and he that soweth discord among brethren."

God hates these seven things. Therefore, when we are talking about the *Seven Levels of Promise for the Overcomer*, we cannot talk just about all the great things with number seven in the Bible. Seven is the number of divine perfection, but these verse point out seven things that God does not like—seven things that God hates.

First of all, God does not like a proud look, the look that conveys the attitude, "I do not need God. I do not need anybody; I can do it all by myself." While there is power in one individual devoted to God, we also have to realize that not only are we dependent upon God, but He has put others around us for a reason. He hates a proud or an arrogant type of look that broadcasts the philosophy of "me, myself, and I." That negative pride says I do not care what God has to say.

The second thing that God hates is a lying tongue. The Book of Revelation clearly states that no liar will make it into the kingdom of Heaven. God hates lying, and if God hates lying, we should certainly hate lying.

Third, God hates hands that shed innocent blood. When Cain killed Abel, the blood of Abel cried out from the ground. The blood speaks, and God hates the shedding of innocent blood. The Book of Revelation shows that God hears the cry of the blood of martyred saints, the cry for vengeance, for righteousness, and for justice to be done.

The fourth thing God hates is a heart that devises wicked imaginations. God does not like for us to imagine evil. This does not only refer to those who plot to blow up buildings, or who strap bombs onto themselves, walk into crowded areas and detonate the bombs, taking out as many people as they can, all in the name of God. This also refers to people who may not kill physically, but who kill with their tongues, mutilating the hearts and spirits of others, even their own children, by telling them, "You are no good; you will never amount to anything." The wicked imagination that fosters this kind of hateful speech is what God hates. We have to cast down imaginations and all of the high things that exalt themselves against the knowledge of God.

Fifth, God hates feet that are swift in running to mischief, to foolishness, to trouble, and to negative things. God wants us to run to the Redeemer. He wants us to run to the Savior. He wants us to run to the arms of Jesus and not run to mischief and trouble.

The sixth thing God hates is a false witness who speaks lies. Earlier we looked at the seven witnesses to Christ in the Gospel of John. Well, God does not want us to be a false witness. The seven witnesses to Christ in John's Gospel were positive witnesses to the fact that Jesus is the Son of God.

A false witness is one who speaks lies. When we say, for instance, "Jesus is the Son of God," but then live a life that does not back that up, we become witnesses who do not speak truth, but who live lives of lies. Even though many are speaking a truth on one hand, they are declaring a lie on the other, claiming that the Bible is true, but not allowing it to be true in their own lives. God hates a false witness; we need to be a positive witness.

We overcome Satan, according to Revelation 12:11: *"by the blood of the Lamb, and by the word of [our] testimony."* Our testimony is extremely important. If we want to overcome Satan, we must do so through the blood of Jesus and through the word of our testimony—our *positive* witness for Christ.

Finally, the seventh thing God hates is he that sows discord among brothers—people who cause disunity. There is supposed to be unity in the church, in the body of Christ. People should be able to look at the church and tell by our unity and love for one another that God is real and that Christ is alive. As the body of Christ on earth, we, the church, represent Him before a watching world. We must, therefore, be very careful of the example we set and the witness we give.

There is a lot of truth in the old song that says, "You are the only Jesus that some will ever see; you are the only Bible that some will ever read." We are supposed to show people the love of God that He has poured out in our hearts (Romans 5:5). Wherever the love of God holds sway, unity is one of the fruits. Disunity is of the devil. God does not like those who sow seeds of discord among the brethren. We always reap what we sow, and if we sow seeds of discord, then we will reap a harvest of discord in our soul and in our life.

4.) Getting Up After The Seventh Fall

✝ **Proverbs 24:16:**

"For a just man falleth seven times, and riseth up again: but the wicked shall fall into mischief."

This Scripture always makes me think of Jesus, a just man, the Son of the living God, the Redeemer of humanity, who shed His blood for us seven times.

There are many times in life where the pressure is on us, and where we may fall into difficult situations. After Jesus died, many of His disciples thought He had fallen in defeat. They had believed that He was going to overthrow the Roman government and liberate Israel, but now He was dead, and they had forsaken Him. Jesus rose in complete and total victory. After He was crucified, He rose from the dead, breaking forever the once inescapable grip of death on humanity.

Jesus' enemies thought they had beaten Him. Even as He hung on the cross, they mocked Him, saying, "If you're the Son of God, why don't you come down from the cross?" As John recorded, seven people had declared that He was the Son of

God, but now He was dying. Yet despite all His enemies did to Him, Jesus rose again, defeating death forever. That is the key. A just man can fall seven times and rise up each time, but the wicked will fall and be destroyed. They will fall and not rise up again.

The truly righteous will always rise again after a fall. We can be in situation where it seems like we have fallen. But where we have failed, where we have faltered, where it seems like we are ineffective, God really is using those circumstances as a set up to bring us to another level of effectiveness, another level of service.

5.) Seven Times Hotter

Chapter three of the Book of Daniel tells the story of Shadrach, Meshach and Abednego, and how they defied King Nebuchadnezzar's order to worship a golden image. In rage, the king commanded that the three young Jewish men be thrown into a fiery furnace that had been heated seven times hotter than normal.

This is another Scripture that shows how perils can sometimes accompany the number seven. But it is also a beautiful and powerful story of overcoming. The soldiers that threw the young men into the furnace were killed by the excessive heat, yet Shadrach, Meshach, and Abednego were unharmed. They had determined that they were not going to bow down to King Nebuchadnezzar's image, but would remain true and worship only their God—the one true God. As the king looked on to observe their fate, he saw a fourth man walking around in the fiery furnace—the Son of God, protecting the three young men.

Even after the furnace is heated up seven times hotter in your life, Jesus still is able to move. In addition, we have to realize that the enemy will try to use this number seven. Remember the seven sons of Sceva in the book of Acts, who tried to cast out a demon in Jesus' name, without being followers of Jesus. The demon replied, *"Paul I know, and Jesus I know, but who are you?"* Satan will always try to counterfeit things that he knows are up in Heaven. This is the reason why we have to get that spiritual connection and significance and genuine touch from God, so we will understand that He gives us the power to be overcomers.

6.) What Do You See

✝ Zechariah 4:2:

"And he said unto me, What seest thou? And I said, I have looked, and behold a candlestick all of gold, with a bowl upon the top of it, and his seven lamps thereon, and seven pipes to the seven lamps which are upon the top thereof."

The angel asked Zechariah, *"What seest thou?"* We have to learn how to see with the vision that God supernaturally gives us. Human vision is important, but we need to go beyond that and ask God to give us a new level of faith, a measure of faith where, in the midst of some of the most perplexing situations, God can say to us, "What do you see?" We need to learn how to see the candlestick that God gives to bring light, and to see the bowl that has oil that is connected to the lamps and the pipes that are connected to it, for God's oil to flow.

Hebrews 11:30 says, *"By faith the walls of Jericho fell down, after they were compassed about seven days."* Joshua at the battle of Jericho had the children of Israel march around the walls seven times, and it was after that seventh time that they blew the trumpets, and the walls of Jericho fell flat.

There is power in our shout. There is power in our trumpeting. There is power in our heralding. But there also comes a time of quietness when we need to walk about a situation; when we need to speak forth God's Word, yet at the same time, go forth quietly and walk until the time comes for us to shout and blow our trumpets. The shout and trumpet blast of the church need to mean something, because the trumpet sound of Jesus means something.

When He cracks the eastern sky and blows His trumpet, we are all going to be caught up to meet Him in the air. Well, our shout should mean something in our communities, in our society, in our families in the midst of the pressures of life that is going on. We have so many situations in our communities where our young men and young women are being imprisoned at younger and younger ages. When I go into the prisons I see young ladies bringing children to visit a young man who hasn't even reached the age of twenty-one yet, but who is locked behind bars.

We have to wake up and see the relevance of God's Word, *the Seven Levels of Promise for the Overcomer*, and apply it to our lives each day. Every day we need to stand on God's Word, just as they did in the Civil Rights Movement, because they knew there were things that needed to be overcome. We have to realize that the struggle continues. Let us never forgot the deep heartfelt meaning of Charles Wesley's great hymn entitled, "A Charge To Keep I Have"

> A charge to keep I have,
> A God to glorify,
> A never-dying soul to save,
> And fit it for the sky.
>
> To serve the present age,
> My calling to fulfill:
> O may it all my powers engage
> To do my Master's will!
>
> Arm me with jealous care,
> As in Thy sight to live;
> And O Thy servant, Lord, prepare
> A strict account to give!

Help me to watch and pray,

And on Thyself rely,

Assured, if I my trust betray,

I shall forever die.[46]

If you think the Civil Rights Movement is over, then you are ignorant. We have to realize that injustice still exists. There is still discrimination against all different races, cultures, communities, including the Christian community. Great injustices are done every day, seven days a week. We have to come together as never before. Realizing that the revelation is relevant, we have to apply it seven days of the week. We have to apply it twelve months of the year, we have to go after it

---

[46] A Charge To Keep I Have, Charles Wesley, *Short Hymns on Select Passages of Holy Scripture*, 1762. Music: Boylston, Lowell Mason, *The Choir, or Union Collection of Church Music*, 1832

24/7. General George S. Patton stated: "You need to overcome the tug of people against you as you reach for high goals."[47]

7.) Seven Attributes To Add To Your Faith

✝ **2 Peter 1:5-9:**

"And beside this, giving all diligence, add to your faith virtue; and to virtue knowledge; And to knowledge temperance; and to temperance patience; and to patience godliness; And to godliness brotherly kindness; and to brotherly kindness charity. For if these things be in you, and abound, they make you that ye shall neither be barren nor unfruitful in the knowledge of our Lord Jesus Christ. But he that lacketh these things is blind, and cannot see afar off, and hath forgotten that he was purged from his old sins."

This passage is very powerful, because it says that we need to add to our faith seven things:

1. Virtue
2. Knowledge
3. Temperance
4. Patience

---

[47] General George S. Patton concerning overcoming and high goals

5. Godliness

6. Brotherly kindness

7. Charity

We need each of these seven points in addition to our faith. God's Word clearly says that if we do not have these seven points, our lives will become barren. We become unfruitful in the knowledge of Jesus Christ. When we lack these seven points in addition to our faith, we become spiritually blind. We cannot see afar off. We will not have the vision that God needs us to have to do the things He has called us to do.

The Seven Powerful P's

Rev. Frances W. Mackey Hull

The Rev. Dr. Frances W. Mackey Hull of Lakeland, Florida, in her message entitled, "Strength is the Solid Stuff that Believers are Made Of," refers to "the seven Powerful P's": the power of prayer, the power of promptness, the power of perseverance, the power of politeness, the power of preparedness, the power of purity, and the power of patience. As she touched upon these seven P's, I thought about her life. She was raised in Woodford, Virginia. She gave her life to Christ as a very young child. The Lord began to use her through her church in Virginia, where Rev. Bray was the pastor. When she was growing up there was a little child that was sick unto death, and she prayed that the Lord would heal the child. My mother laid hands on the child, and the Lord actually healed the child. As my mother grew up, she went through many hard things, yet she learned the seven P's.

With some help, my mother went to Virginia Union University in Richmond, Virginia, where she focused in the area of Christian education.

When my mother met my father, Rev. Arthur Mackey, Sr., who lived across the campus of Virginia Union University, he said, "Lord, I want that!" The Lord blessed the two of them to come together. Years later they would get married, and my sister Frances, my other sister Vivian, and myself soon came on the scene. It all came about through a relationship with God and the power of those seven P's: the prayer, the promptness, the perseverance, the politeness, the preparedness, the purity, and the patience. Like my father, she grew up in utter poverty, but there was love in the home. There was care in the home. There was sharing in the home. That love made a world of difference. Now she travels around the world preaching the Gospel of Jesus Christ, letting people know that strength is the stuff that Christians are made of. The seven P's made a world of difference.

She was married to my father until his death on October 29, 1999. She served as First Lady of Mt. Sinai Baptist Church Cathedral where I serve as pastor now, for 35 years. She still is a very faithful long distance member of the church. Today she has remarried, to the Bishop Arthur Hull of New Jersey, and they are going forth in ministry.

The Classic Seven Promises of a Promise Keeper

Before my father passed away, he and I attended an event sponsored by the Promise Keepers, held on the National Mall in Washington, D.C. The Promise Keepers affirm the Seven Promises of a Promise Keeper:

1. A man and his God

2. A man and his mentors

3. A man and his integrity;

4. A man and his family

5. A man and his church

6. A man and his brothers

7. A man and his world.

We were both supportive of this movement, and believed it to be a great move of God. I was serving as assistant pastor at that time, and we went down to Washington, D.C. and led a delegation down there as well, as many pastors did. All the churches came together for this great meeting. My father and I were both wearing purple clergy collars and dark suits. Outside the Mall was a women's group, a group of feminist protesters. They did not realize that my father was a great Civil Rights leader, and a great human rights leader, and that we both fight for women's rights, and for the rights of people that are discriminated against. All they saw was that we were going to a Promise Keeper's rally and they assumed that we must have been a bunch of sexist pigs. They began booing us, and throwing things at us, and belittling us. We just stayed focused and walked into the meeting.

When we got into the Promise Keepers meeting, a group of men, recognizing us as two preachers, began to cheer us. I was pushing one of my friends, Karl Dresler, who was in a wheelchair, and they were just elated to see us in the meeting. They began to pray for us, and to embrace us. In a matter of moments we had moved from one extreme to another.

I still think of that event and the way we all got down on our knees and prayed to God. It is still hard to imagine how many men there were; they stretched as far as the eye could see, and I believe that that was a seed for revival in this nation, and throughout this world.

This all really hit home as we were preparing to come back to New York. There at the train station, men just began to pray, shout, and sing. The spirit of worship just spread through the place, and there were hundreds of people there to catch the Amtrak. It was an awesome witness of the power of God.

Father I Stretch My Hands to Thee

The great executive, Mary Kay Ash, said, "God does not ask your ability, or your inability, He asks only your availability." God is looking for people who will say, "Lord, I am available to you. Father, I stretch my hands to you. I need you, God, as never before."

Charles Wesley

"Father, I Stretch My Hands to Thee" is one of the many beloved hymns written by the Methodist leader and hymn writer Charles Wesley, who wrote more than 7,000 hymns. More than 5,500 of them were published and entered into worldwide distribution. This hymn was the classic Christian hymn that Rev. John Downes called out on Friday, November 4, 1774, when death literally came upon him in West Street Chapel, London. Charles Wesley was greatly inspired by Rev. Downes' ministry. The afternoon before his last sermon, Rev. Downes stated, 'I feel such a love to the people of West Street, that I would be content to die with them. I do not find myself very well; but I must be with them this evening.' His sermon text for that particular day was "Come unto Me, all ye that labour and are heavy laden." An awesome anointing came upon the Gospel message; but after speaking for only ten minutes, with his strength almost gone, he declared the words written by Charles Wesley, "Father, I stretch my hands to Thee, No other help I know."

Rev. Downes' voice began to fail him. He literally fell to his knees, as if to pray. The clergy who were present picked him up and put him in bed, where he breathed his very last breath on this side of glory. Rev. John Downes was only fifty-two.

Don't wait for the funeral home hearse to bring you to church. Cry out right now those very words no matter what you are going through:

> Father, I stretch my hands to Thee,
>
> No other help I know;
>
> If Thou withdraw Thyself from me,
>
> Ah! whither shall I go?[48]

In the next chapter I want to look at the seven feasts of Israel and relate them to the *Seven Levels of Promise for the Overcomer*, as outlined in the book of Revelation, especially in

---

[48] Father, I Stretch My Hands to Thee—Words: Charles Wesley, A Collection of Songs and Hymns, 1741. Music: Naomi, Hans G. Nägeli, arranged by Lowell Mason, 1836.

chapters two and three. The parallels are amazing. It is truly remarkable to see the correlation between the seven feasts of Israel and the seven promises that are given to each of the churches.

Notes For The Overcomer

CHAPTER SIX

Seven Parallels Between the Seven Feasts and the Seven Churches

S even parallels exist between the seven feasts of Israel and Christ's messages to the seven churches in the Book of Revelation. Studying the seven feasts can help us to better understand the seven messages to the seven churches, because God establishes the end from the beginning[0].

The Seven Feasts of Israel

The seven feasts of Israel are laid out in the 23rd chapter of the Book of Leviticus. They are:

1. The Feast of Passover (Leviticus 23:1-5).
2. The Feast of Unleavened Bread (Leviticus 23:6-8).
3. The Feast of the First Fruits (Leviticus 23:9-14).
4. The Feast of Weeks (better known to us as Pentecost—50 days after Passover; Leviticus 23:15-22).

5. The Feast of Trumpets (Leviticus 23:23-25).

6. The Feast of the Day of Atonement (Leviticus 23:26-32).

7. The Feast of Tabernacles (Leviticus 23:33-44).

Here are the Passages Explained in Relation to the *Seven Levels of Promise for the Overcomer*

The Feast of Passover

Leviticus 23:1-5:

"And the LORD spake unto Moses, saying, Speak unto the children of Israel, and say unto them, concerning the feasts of the LORD, which ye shall proclaim to be holy convocations, even these are my feasts. Six days shall work be done: but the seventh day is the Sabbath of rest, a holy convocation; ye shall do no work therein: it is the Sabbath of the LORD in all your dwellings. These are the feasts of the LORD, even holy convocations, which ye shall proclaim in their seasons. In the fourteenth day of the first month at even is the LORD'S Passover."

As the *first* of the First Month feasts, Passover commemorates the Israelites' liberation from slavery and Egypt, and foreshadows the first coming of Jesus Christ, the Ultimate Overcomer. The first Passover event is described in Exodus chapters 12 and 13, while God's specific instructions for its annual observance are found in Leviticus chapter 23. Passover represents God's deliverance from sin's bondage, which was accomplished, once and for all, through the death of Christ.

The Passover lamb, which foreshadowed Jesus' finished work on the cross was prepared and sacrificed. In Egypt, on that first Passover, the Israelites daubed lamb's blood on the doorposts and lintels of their houses so the Death Angel would "pass over" them. That same night, all the firstborn of the Egyptians died, but the Israelites were spared and delivered.

Passover was celebrated each year until Jesus Christ, the Lamb of God, died, thereby fulfilling Passover and rendering it obsolete. The salvation typified in the Passover was fulfilled in Jesus' life, death, and resurrection. He became our Passover (Pesach) Lamb, establishing a new covenant in His blood at the Last Supper (Passover meal).

For Christian believers, Passover speaks of the power of Jesus' precious blood to save us from sin. Indeed, it speaks of true salvation for all believers in Yeshua, Jesus Christ, the Ultimate Overcomer, our beloved Messiah. As fulfilled in Christ, Passover heralds the beginning of new life in Him; old things pass away, and all things become new. Everyone who receives Jesus, as Lord and Savior experiences the Passover, which is being ransomed from death by the blood of Jesus.

The Feast of Unleavened Bread

Leviticus 23:6-8:

"And on the fifteenth day of the same month is the feast of unleavened bread unto the LORD: seven days ye must eat unleavened bread. In the first day ye shall have an holy convocation: ye shall do no servile work therein. But ye shall offer an offering made by fire unto the LORD seven days: in the seventh day is an holy convocation: ye shall do no servile work therein."

For the Feast of Unleavened Bread, the Israelites removed all yeast and leaven from their households. These things symbolized sin and uncleanness. The Jews had to remove every trace of yeast from the house before they could celebrate this feast.

Unleavened bread signifies the purification work of the Holy Spirit to remove sin from our lives. After leaving Egypt, Israel passed through the Red Sea; they went down through the waters, and Egypt was cut off forever.

The Red Sea experience was a type of baptism for Israel. Likewise for us, the Feast of Unleavened Bread literally speaks of sin being removed from the believer's life. It is symbolized in the ordinance of baptism, where, just as Jesus died, was buried, and was raised to life, so the person who believes in Yeshua, Jesus, is buried to his old way of life and resurrected to a new life in Jesus. The removal of leaven also speaks of the removal of corruption and heretical or erroneous religious doctrines from the believer's life.

This is the ongoing work of the Holy Spirit as He purifies us from sin, hypocrisy, legalism, denying the miraculous – in other words, getting Egypt out of us! Israel was delivered from Egypt, and after we have been saved the next step in our salvation is water baptism, which purifies us of a guilty conscience and symbolizes getting Egypt out of us.

The Feast of Firstfruits

Leviticus 23:9-14:

"And the LORD spake unto Moses, saying, Speak unto the children of Israel, and say unto them, When ye be come into the land which I give unto you, and shall reap the harvest thereof, then ye shall bring a sheaf of the firstfruits of your harvest unto the priest: And he shall wave the sheaf before the LORD, to be accepted for you: on the morrow after the Sabbath the priest shall wave it. And ye shall offer that day when ye wave the sheaf an he lamb without blemish of the first year for a burnt offering unto the LORD. And the meat offering thereof shall be two tenth deals of fine flour mingled with oil, an offering made by fire unto the LORD for a sweet savour: and the drink offering thereof shall be of wine, the fourth part of an hin. And ye shall eat neither bread, nor parched corn, nor green ears, until the selfsame day that ye have brought an offering unto your God: it shall be a statute for ever throughout your generations in all your dwellings."

298

The Feast of Firstfruits, which involved the waving of the sheaves before God, symbolized God's acceptance of His people through Jesus Christ's precious blood. This means that Jesus Christ's blood was made an atonement for us. In the greatest demonstration of God's "amazing grace," Jesus Christ became our mediator before the Heavenly Father; His death atoned for our sins, and through His resurrection, He became the firstfruit from the dead.

These first three feasts symbolically correspond to the "outer court" of the Tabernacle of Moses. In the Old Covenant "outer court" experience, there was the bronze altar, symbolizing the shedding of blood—the sacrifice for our sin. Sin was judged there with the blood of bulls and goats, just as sin was judged at the cross with the shedding of Jesus' blood. Then the priests would move to the brass laver, which speaks of cleansing from our daily walk in this world. It also represents "the washing of the water by the word," which would be a type of baptism or cleansing before we enter the Holy Place.

Experiencing these first three feasts could be compared to the 30-fold increase, but it is not a stopping place in our Christian walk.

The Feast of Weeks (Pentecost)

Leviticus 23:15-22:

"And ye shall count unto you from the morrow after the Sabbath, from the day that ye brought the sheaf of the wave offering; seven Sabbaths shall be complete: Even unto the morrow after the seventh Sabbath shall ye number fifty days; and ye shall offer a new meat offering unto the LORD. Ye shall bring out of your habitations two wave loaves of two tenth deals: they shall be of fine flour; they shall be baken with leaven; they are the firstfruits unto the LORD. And ye shall offer with the bread seven lambs without blemish of the first year, and one young bullock, and two rams: they shall be for a burnt offering unto the LORD, with their meat offering, and their drink offerings, even an offering made by fire, of sweet savour unto the LORD. Then ye shall sacrifice one kid of the goats for a sin offering, and two lambs of the first year for a sacrifice of peace offerings. And the priest shall wave them with the bread of the firstfruits for a wave offering before the LORD, with the two lambs: they shall be holy to the LORD for the priest. And ye shall proclaim on the selfsame day, that it may be an holy convocation unto

you: ye shall do no servile work therein: it shall be a statute for ever in all your dwellings throughout your generations. And when ye reap the harvest of your land, thou shalt not make clean riddance of the corners of thy field when thou reapest, neither shalt thou gather any gleaning of thy harvest: thou shalt leave them unto the poor, and to the stranger: I am the LORD your God."

As a Third Month feast, the Feast of Weeks (or Pentecost) was a wilderness feast that originated at Mt. Sinai as a secondary experience with God after the feasts of the first month. God did a new thing. Exodus chapter 19 describes the circumstances surrounding this feast. Acts chapter 2 details its New Testament counterpart, where on the Day of Pentecost God did a new thing by sending His Holy Spirit to dwell in the hearts of His children.

God told Israel to prepare themselves because He would come down to speak to them audibly. He did so at Mount Sinai, accompanied by thunder, lightning, wind, fire on the top of the mountain, and thick clouds of darkness over the mountain. The coming down of the Lord on to the mountain was heralded by a very long trumpet (shofar) blast. After fifty days in the wilderness, God's glory came down. The Feast of Weeks commemorated this event and celebrated the "early rain" harvest which included the wheat, corn, and barley.

Fifty days after the death and resurrection of Jesus Christ, the 120 believers who waited in the upper room in Jerusalem experienced the coming of the Holy Spirit on the Day of Pentecost (harvest celebration). The room was filled with the sound of a mighty rushing wind, cloven tongues of fire sat upon their heads, and the room shook. As the Spirit gave them utterance, the apostles spoke in new tongues to proclaim Christ in the native languages of all those from all the nations who had gathered in Jerusalem for the festival.

People from all the surrounding nations had gathered in Jerusalem, and God came to them in a new way. This was a secondary experience with the Lord after salvation. The 120 believers were all baptized in the Holy Spirit. Today, the Holy Spirit can speak directly to individual believers, just as when God came down on the mountain to speak with Israel, only now He resides within us.

A great harvest of souls took place on that Day of Pentecost. Just as the Feast of Weeks speaks of the early rain with the wheat, corn and barley harvest, 3000 new believers—an "early rain" harvest—were added to the body of Christ. That number soon grew to 5000, and then continued to multiply as new believers were added daily.

The apostle Peter explained to the crowd on that day, that the phenomenon they were witnessing was the fulfillment of Joel's prophecy that in the last days, God would pour out His Spirit on all flesh. In other words, the "last days" began on the Day of Pentecost, and continue until now.

This feast may be compared to the "Holy Place" in the Tabernacle of Moses, where gifts were given and the illumination of the Holy Spirit took place with the lampstand and the table of showbread.

A believer who experiences Pentecost may be compared to receiving the 60-fold increase, but once again, we are not to camp at Pentecost. Israel was told to leave the mountain and journey on toward Canaan. Likewise, we must also continue on in our walk, pressing into the full light of day and the full revelation of the glory of God.

From the fourth to the sixth month there was no rain, and no other prescribed feasts. Symbolically, this speaks of the Dark Ages, when the light of the Gospel nearly went out in the earth.

Many plagues broke out during this time, and there was very little knowledge of the Word of God. This dark period lasted until Martin Luther came along in the 1500's with the truth of "Salvation by Grace." In the next few centuries, little by little, truths were being restored to the body of Christ, and many of the historic revivals broke out with Finney, Wesley, and many others.

It was not until the Azusa Street Revival in the early 1900's did we see an escalation of truth, and power and visitation of the Holy Spirit once again upon the church. It was almost as though the prophetic clock stopped during the Dark Ages, and resumed as we approached the 20th century.

The Feast of Trumpets

Leviticus 23:23-25:

"And the LORD spake unto Moses, saying, Speak unto the children of Israel, saying, In the seventh month, in the first day of the month, shall ye have a Sabbath, a memorial of blowing of trumpets, an holy convocation. Ye shall do no servile work therein: but ye shall offer an offering made by fire unto the LORD."

With the arrival of the Feast of Trumpets, also known as Rosh Hashanah, we enter into the highly significant trio of the Seventh Month feasts, which include also the Day of Atonement (Yom Kippur) and the Feast of Tabernacles (Booths). These are autumn feasts that speak of the second coming of Jesus Christ, the Ultimate Overcomer, at the end of the age. Blowing of the shofar (ram's horn trumpet) announced both the beginning of the feast and the soon arrival of the great Day of Atonement (a 10-day period of time as described in Numbers Chapter 10).

Also known as the Days of Awe, it was a time of repentance and reflection on the previous year. On the Jewish calendar it was known as the "Head of the Year" (New Year), and its time was determined by the new moon. The Feast of Trumpets was a two-day feast 10symbolizing the fact that no one knows the day or the hour of the Lord's coming. It speaks of trial, testing, affliction, and sifting to get the sin out of our lives. The New Testament likens this to the image of wood, hay, and stubble being burned out of our lives through affliction, and of pride being burned out of our lives in order to produce repentance and the purifying and perfecting of our lives through the work of the Holy Spirit. All of this is appropriate as the Day of Atonement (Yom Kippur) approaches—ten days after the Feast of Trumpets.

The trumpets speak of prophetic voices on the Earth – healing, restoration, new worship being released with new songs of the Lord. Trumpets called together a solemn assembly, which served to produce spiritual unity and break down walls of separation in the body. A good example of this today is shown in what is happening with conferences in the last 20 years. The body of Christ is assembling across denominational lines in large gatherings together all over the world. At the same time, Israel is hearing the trumpet call to return to their homeland, and many are coming to the knowledge of salvation through "Yeshua"—Jesus, as their Messiah. Trumpets are being sounded throughout the earth, resulting in end time events being fulfilled just as Scripture prophesied.

The Feast of Trumpets represents a calling and preparing of Israel and the church in the last days for Jesus' return and the climax of the ages.

The Day of Atonement

Leviticus 23:26-32:

"And the LORD spake unto Moses, saying, Also on the tenth day of this seventh month there shall be a day of atonement: it shall be an holy convocation unto you; and ye shall afflict your souls, and offer an offering made by fire unto the LORD. And ye shall do no work in that same day: for it is a day of atonement, to make an atonement for you before the LORD your God. For whatsoever soul it be that shall not be afflicted in that same day, he shall be cut off from among his people. And whatsoever soul it be that doeth any work in that same day, the same soul will I destroy from among his people. Ye shall do no manner of work: it shall be a statute for ever throughout your generations in all your dwellings. It shall be unto you a Sabbath of rest, and ye shall afflict your souls: in the ninth day of the month at even, from even unto even, shall ye celebrate your Sabbath."

The Day of Atonement (Yom Kippur) was "legally" accomplished by the shedding of Jesus' blood, but has not taken place experientially yet. Yom Kippur was a day of national cleansing for Israel, a time of corporate cleansing in which the high priest would enter the Holy of Holies and sprinkle blood seven times on the mercy seat to atone for the sins of the people. The high priest wore linen cloth and carried a censer full of smoking incense behind the veil.

Two goats were also used: one as a sin offering, and the other as the "scapegoat" that would be released into the wilderness, symbolically bearing the sins of the people, and carrying their sins away.

Yom Kippur was not a feast day, but a day of fasting. A solemn fast was declared for twenty-four hours. No manner of work was to be done. It was a Sabbath to the Lord.

In the church age, the Day of Atonement speaks of the removing of iniquity, carnality, and sin from the body of Christ; removing our sin nature, and perfecting us so we will be a pure and spotless Bride of Christ, adorned and ready to meet our Bridegroom.

Also known as the "Day of Perfection," Yom Kippur speaks of the appearance of the Lord Jesus. The incense represents the sacrifice of His body and blood. In one day there would be cleansing. This observance also speaks of worship in fullness—a drawing back of the veil to see Christ as He really is. It has to do with the sanctification process—the cleansing and removal of filth from our lives through affliction.

The Feast of Tabernacles

Leviticus 23:33-44:

"And the LORD spake unto Moses, saying, Speak unto the children of Israel, saying, The fifteenth day of this seventh month shall be the feast of tabernacles for seven days unto the LORD. On the first day shall be an holy convocation: ye shall do no servile work therein. Seven days ye shall offer an offering made by fire unto the LORD: on the eighth day shall be an holy convocation unto you; and ye shall offer an offering made by fire unto the LORD: it is a solemn assembly; and ye shall do no servile work therein. These are the feasts of the LORD, which ye shall proclaim to be holy convocations, to offer an offering made by fire unto the LORD, a burnt offering, and a meat offering, a sacrifice, and drink offerings, every thing upon his day: Beside the Sabbaths of the LORD, and beside your gifts, and beside all your vows, and beside all your freewill offerings, which ye give unto the LORD. Also in the fifteenth day of the seventh month, when ye have gathered in the fruit of the land, ye shall keep a feast unto the LORD seven days: on the first day shall be a Sabbath, and on the eighth day shall be a

Sabbath. And ye shall take you on the first day the boughs of goodly trees, branches of palm trees, and the boughs of thick trees, and willows of the brook; and ye shall rejoice before the LORD your God seven days. And ye shall keep it a feast unto the LORD seven days in the year. It shall be a statute for ever in your generations: ye shall celebrate it in the seventh month. Ye shall dwell in booths seven days; all that are Israelites born shall dwell in booths: That your generations may know that I made the children of Israel to dwell in booths, when I brought them out of the land of Egypt: I am the LORD your God. And Moses declared unto the children of Israel the feasts of the LORD."

Known also as the Feast of Ingathering, the Feast of Tabernacles was a Canaan land feast, celebrated after Israel inherited the Promise Land after 40 years of wilderness wanderings. For seven days the Israelites lived in booths made of leafy branches to commemorate their journey in the wilderness. Ingathering was a feast of glory, the "latter rains" harvest of the fruit, the wheat, the oil, and the wine. From the

New Testament perspective, it is a Feast of Light celebrating the arrival of Jesus, the Light of the World.

The Feast of Tabernacles speaks of a victorious Bride: New Covenant believers have repeated what Israel did. Israel wandered for forty years in the wilderness, and the church has "wandered" for forty Jubilees: 2000 years since the birth of Jesus. This day speaks of the revealing of God's glory—the revealing of "the Father"—and of the drawing back of the veil for the full revelation of God. It speaks of signs, wonders, and worldwide harvest (Hebrews 12:22). It speaks to the fulfillment of the ages, when the reaper will overtake the sower with a massive harvest of souls. The early and the latter rains will come together, resulting in more people getting saved than in all of previous history combined.

On the last day of the feast, the pouring of the pitchers of water represented God's Spirit poured out in fullness. It would culminate with a Feast of Illumination, where the Jews would come with torches, and the temple would be greatly illuminated. This speaks of the Utimate Overcomer, Jesus Christ, the Light of the World.

The Feast of Tabernacles speaks of a completion of the ages and the revealing of our Bridegroom. It speaks of entering into the Holy of Holies as compared with the Tabernacle of Moses – the 100-fold believer who has gone on to perfection by allowing the full working of the Holy Spirit in their lives. It speaks of intimate communion and the revealing of our Lord in the fullness of His glory.

Passover in Relation to the Seven Levels of Promise for the Overcomer

Let us take a closer look at these seven feasts, particularly as they relate to the *seven levels of promise for the overcomer*.

The Feast of Passover in Relation to the Seven Levels of Promise for the Overcomer

Most of us are familiar with the story of the Passover. God had sent the plagues upon Egypt, and Pharaoh would not let the children of Israel go. The last plague was the death of the firstborn in every household that did not have lamb's blood on the doorpost. In obedience to Moses' instructions (which he received from God), each family in Israel killed a lamb, and put blood upon their doorpost so the Death Angel would pass over their home and not bring death. The firstborn in every other house in Egypt died, including Pharaoh's firstborn. Therefore, the Feast of Passover, the shedding of the blood of the lamb, the covering of the blood of the lamb on the doorpost of the home, and brings about the Feast of Passover.

In Revelation 2:1-7, as we have seen, Christ addresses the church in Ephesus, criticizing them for the fault of leaving their first love. He called them to remember from where they were fallen, to repent, and to return to their first works, lest He come quickly and remove their candlestick. Of course, the candlestick is symbolic of the church. He goes on to say that if they would overcome and deal with the temptations, the trials, and the ups and downs that they were facing, they would not be hurt in the second death.

Death occurred in large numbers during that very first Passover, when the last plague came upon Egypt because of Pharaoh's obstinacy in refusing to release the children of Israel. In relation to Jesus' promises to the seven churches, overcomers are the ones who apply the blood of the Lamb to their hearts, to the doorposts of their lives, and to the situations, problems and predicaments of life. If they do this, they will not be hurt in the second death.

Earlier in the book, I explained that this means that one who accepts Jesus Christ as Lord and Savior does not have to worry about eternal separation from God when death comes. True born again believers will never be hurt in the second death, because they possess eternal life in Christ.

The church in Ephesus had left their first love. There were those in Ephesus who called themselves Jews but did not live out the true meaning of Judaism. Of course, there were many real people of Jewish integrity. Jesus was a Jewish brother, as were Peter and Paul. These were men of great integrity, men of great faith, meant to be greatly honored, but Jesus realized that there were those who called themselves Jews, who were not doing what they should be doing, just like there are those who call themselves Christians who really are not doing what they should be doing. These people were blasphemous, and Jesus Christ said that they were of the synagogue of Satan.

So leaving your first love brings you from the synagogue of the saints to the synagogue of Satan. It brings you from the system of the Savior to the system of Satan. When you stay away from your first love long enough, you can get a second love, and even a third love. Directly or indirectly, you enter into an affair with Satan. Christ wants us to return to and to retain our first love—our undiluted and undivided love for Him.

Those who leave their first love and get involved with the synagogue of Satan, if they do not overcome, will be hurt in the second death. In other words, they will not have eternal life with Jesus Christ, but they will have eternal condemnation in hell. Everyone has eternal life, but the key question is, where are we going to spend this eternal life?

The second church, the suffering church of Smyrna, actually ties in literally to all of the feasts of Israel, because the Jewish people are suffering and will continue to suffer until Jesus Christ, the Suffering Servant, the Wounded Healer, comes Himself, and sets up His kingdom in Jerusalem. Throughout the ages, Jews worldwide have faced great persecution for practicing their faith. The greatest example of this is, of course, the Holocaust, under Hitler and the Nazi regime in Germany. Likewise, Christians have suffered persecution for their faith, as well, in every generation.

The Feast of Unleavened Bread in Relation to the Seven Levels of Promise for the Overcomer

Now let us dig in deeper and look at the second feast of Israel, which is the Feast of Unleavened Bread. One of the key words there is "bread." In addition, let us look at the third church that is mentioned in the *Seven Levels of Promise of the Overcomer.*

The third church that Jesus addressed was the church of Pergamos. He spoke to them as the Bread of Life, who also had the sharp two-edged sword. Jesus, the Ultimate Overcomer, speaks to them of the place where Satan's seat is. In other words, evil in Pergamos had progressed not only to the point of being a synagogue of Satan, but the very seat of Satan. This expresses both the literal reality of what was going on in Pergamos at that time, as well as the figurative and spiritual reality of what was going on in the hearts of the early Christian believers. What was going on in the society, in the secular sense? What was going on in the church in the spiritual sense? Filth and corruption were clearly there, but in the midst of it came the martyrdom of Antipas, who was killed for proclaiming the Gospel of Christ. Antipas was killed "where

Satan dwelleth," where the seat of Satan is, a place where there was a high degree of pagan worship.

Christ told them to repent, or else He would come quickly and fight against them with the sword of His mouth. Nevertheless, He promised that those who overcame would be given hidden manna to eat.

Now what is the second feast of Israel? It is the Feast of Unleavened Bread. Jesus promised hidden manna to the overcomer. The children of Israel had manna that came down from heaven, and in essence, they said, "Well what is this manna? Nevertheless, God has manna that is hidden for those who, like the church of Pergamos, have to deal with the seat of Satan, and with great fornication and idol worship. Don't think that we don't have idol worship today. One of the favorite shows in America today is "American Idol." We make our favorite singers our idols, we make our football players, and our basketball players, and our other athletes idols in our minds. In the midst of this, we have to realize that they are just ordinary people who need God as well. Jesus says that He will give to eat of the hidden manna to the one that overcomes the idolatry of the day and the fornication, the sex outside of marriage, and the negative peer pressure that is prevalent in the world today. This is bread that was not made by the hands of men.

My mother can make some great bread; I mean some *mouth watering* bread! Nobody makes bread better than my mother—except God, who has the hidden manna.

The Feast of First Fruits in Relation to the Seven Levels of Promise for the Overcomer

Now, let us consider the fourth church, the church of Thyatira. Christ speaks to them as the One whose eyes are like a flame of fire, and whose feet are like brass. Jesus knows their charity, their service, and their faith. He knows their patience and their works, and that the last is greater than the first. Nevertheless, they were too tolerant of the spirit of Jezebel, that woman who seduced the servants of God. Therefore, we see a progression from Ephesus, with the synagogue of Satan, to Pergamos, where Satan's seat is, to Thyatira, with the spiritual seduction of the saints with the spirit of Jezebel. Therefore, Satan's seat has come to seduce the saints, which in Revelation

2:24 leads to the "depths of Satan." Even as they speak, they have come into the very depths, and they have known the very depths of Satan. This is the spirit that God wants to be overcome in the church of Thyatira. These things are very much alive today. Sad to say, the seat of Satan thrives in many churches today.

When you go into different states, there is a spirit that is prevalent within each state, or within each country, and you have to enter that state or country pleading the blood of Jesus. Every morning before I go to work, and as I take my children to school, I pray with them, and I plead the blood of Jesus over the school and over the communities, not in fear, but in the power of the Lord. If you look at what happened at Columbine, at Virginia Tech, and at other campuses, it is clear that we must take authority as believers and begin to speak God's Word over the college campuses, the public schools, and the private schools in our community. We must push for our public schools, private schools, and church schools. We must push for our libraries. We must push hard for our communities. We must get involved in the community. We must get out on the streets. We must witness in the community. We must serve in the community. We must get involved on various boards and let the church be the church. We must have an impact, a positive impact in the community. We have to do this because the depths of Satan are prevalent. This is what had to be overcome in Thyatira. Jesus, the Ultimate Overcomer, actually said to the church, that for the ones that would overcome and keep His words to the end, He would give them power over the nations. Power over the nations has a lot to do with being an effective witness for the Lord. The seeds that we have sown in Christ lead to a first fruit in the area of witnessing.

Because Jesus, the Ultimate Overcomer, was the firstborn among many brethren, and because He paid the price of our redemption with His blood, the testimony of Jesus is the Spirit of prophecy. Jesus' life, death, and resurrection set the example of the stand that we ought to take for Christ, and to bear His cross. Moreover, we can begin to see the connection here with the Feast of the First Fruits, or Fruits of the Sheaf, that is brought out in Leviticus.

Christ said of the overcomer, *"And he shall rule them (the nations) with a rod of iron; as the vessels of a potter shall they be broken to shivers: even as I received of My Father. And I will give Him the morning star"* (Rev. 2:27-28). Jesus received of His Father because He was the firstborn among many brethren. He said, *"Father into Thy hand I commend My Spirit."* The sheaves of the first fruit ties in something even deeper here when He says *"I will give you power over the nations."* First fruit means that there is a harvest. Jesus says that *"I will give you power over the nations if you overcome the depths of Satan"* and the spirit of adultery. The spirit of Jezebel wants to be the head of the prophets and to cut off prophetic unction, and anointing, and prophetic flow. It wants to block the flow of the dream and divine destiny of God and desires to seduce the saints and bring them into the depths of Satan, the very depths of degradation. God says He is the one who searches the heart, and He knows where everyone is. God will give the overcomers a true reward. We must not lose our first love, Jesus Christ, as did the church of Ephesus.

Therefore, when we look at the "Seven Levels of Promise for the Overcomer" it ties in directly with the seven feasts of Israel. It is awesome when we realize that power over the nations is a harvest. Overcomers have the power to minister, to reap a harvest of souls, and to rule over them with a rod of iron as the vessel of a potter shall be broken into shivers. When God breaks down a system within a nation, when walls of division are broken, the Gospel is then able to come in. A Christian witness can be established. When the great wall in Berlin came down, the Gospel was able to go into Berlin. Think about all the souls that were saved, all the souls that were harvested into the kingdom. We have to see the connection, and we have to realize that the revelation is relevant.

We must realize that we have to bring the liberating truths of God's Word. God's Word has depth that can transform lives and the revelation is relevant. We must share the Word. We must herald it, because it will bring a great change in the lives of people.

The Feast of Pentecost in Relation to the Seven Levels of Promise for the Overcomer

Now let us consider the Feast of Weeks or the Feast of Pentecost. As I mentioned earlier, the Feast of Pentecost occurs 50 days after Passover. It is the fourth feast of Israel. In conjunction, we need to look at the fourth promise in the *Seven Levels of Promise for the Overcomer*.

We have already dealt with the church of Ephesus, and learned that if they would overcome, they would not be hurt in the second death. What do they need to overcome? Leaving their first love. Overcome people who are a part of the synagogue of Satan. Then we learned that if the church of Pergamos would overcome dwelling where Satan's seat is, and with the spirit of fornication and idolatry, they would eat of the hidden manna. Jesus would give them a white stone wherein their name would be written. To Thyatira, Christ promised that overcomers would receive power over the nations, Jesus would bring about a great harvest and be their morning star.

This brings us to the church of Sardis, to whom Christ spoke, about the seven Spirits of God. We have touched upon the seven Spirits of God earlier, the seven-fold Holy Spirit. The church of Sardis was almost dead, but told to hold fast to that which remained, because there were a few there who had not soiled their garments, but would walk in white for they were worthy. To the overcomer He promised clothing of white raiment and that their names would not be blotted out of the Book of Life. Indeed, He would confess their names before His Father.

When we think of Pentecost, we think of harvest, and when we look at those who are not defiled, it is just like a good harvest that has completely come in and hasn't been spoiled, or corrupted, and this is a reason for great rejoicing. Peter denied Christ three times. Jesus told Peter, *"Satan desires to sift you like wheat,"* but yet Jesus believed in him, Jesus prayed for him, Jesus embraced him, Jesus washed his feet as He washed the feet of the other disciples. Peter denied Jesus three times, yet continued to follow Him from a distance. Jesus restored him on the shore of the Sea of Galilee, and when the Spirit came down on the day of Pentecost, Peter was filled with the Holy Ghost. His garments were washed: those garments which once were defiled and that made him a "cusser"; those garments that brought him to the point of cutting off a slave's ear to prevent Jesus from being arrested. Peter's garments were defiled, but those garments within his heart and soul that were defiled were made clean and were made worthy by the precious blood of the Lamb, which was sprinkled on the Mercy Seat in Heaven.

On the Day of Pentecost, we see one who has been made worthy telling the crowd that 'These men are not drunk. These men are not defiled, but this is that which was spoken by the prophet Joel. That in the last days I will pour out My Spirit on all flesh.' Pentecost and harvest go together, and on that great Day of Pentecost there was a great harvest of 3000 souls. Peter, one who was once defiled; Peter, one who was once not found worthy; Peter, one who was once not considered a great crop; Peter, one who was restored by the Lord and came to greatness, when the Day of Pentecost was fully come, God filled Peter and the rest of the 120 overcoming early Christian believers with the Holy Ghost.

The Feast of Trumpets In Relation to The Seven Levels of Promises for the Overcomer

Now, let us look at the fifth feast of Israel, the Feast of Trumpets, in relation to the *Seven Levels of Promise for the Overcomer*. Jesus had told the church of Sardis to strengthen those things which remained that were ready to die. This is exactly what Jesus had done with His disciples. He took the time to sit down and serve them the last supper, which is known as the Lord's Supper. He took time to wash their feet. He strengthened those things which remained, lest they die. He knew that they would deny Him, but He also knew that if He strengthened those things that remained, they would come back. Judas hung himself, but the other eleven came back.

The Feast of Trumpets relates to the sixth church, the church of Philadelphia. To the church of brotherly love, Christ spoke as the One Who was holy and true, and Who held the key of David. He was the One Who opens doors that no man can shut and shuts doors that no man can open. The message for the ages was being heralded; it was being trumpeted. In addition, Jesus told the church of Philadelphia that He knew their works. He said, *"Behold I have set before you an open door and no man can shut it."* God is heralding this message. This letter is going to be delivered to the church of Philadelphia, that literal congregation, as well as to the church throughout the ages. Jesus tells them that they had a little strength, but had kept His Word. He said, *"You have kept My Word and have not denied My name."* In other words, they had trumpeted the Gospel. They had faithfully heralded it both privately and publicly. They were not ashamed of His Word. He promised that those of the synagogue of Satan would eventually come and worship God at the feet of the Philadelphian believers. Jesus, the

Ultimate Overcomer, knew the church of Philadelphia as true believers. They had a great love for the Lord. Therefore, those who were in the synagogue of Satan were not trumpeting the Truth. Jesus was going to bring them to the feet of those who were truly trumpeting the Truth, that they might truly understand what worship of God is all about.

He talks about them having kept the word of patience, and promised to keep them in the hour of temptation. He talked about them holding fast, and letting no man take their crown. Then He said, *"To the one that overcomes I will make a pillar in the temple of My God, And he shall go no more out, and I will write upon him the name of My God, and the name of a city of My God, which is the New Jerusalem."*

So all of these things are being heralded, all of these things are being trumpeted, all of these things are being declared, and they are being heralded upon those who have been faithful, upon the church of Philadelphia, and not upon a very large congregation, or a very profitable congregation, but upon a very faithful congregation. The lesson for us is that those who hear the trumpet and receive the open door are those who are faithful.

The church of Philadelphia was not very prosperous. They went through hard times, trials, and tribulations, but they remained faithful. The church of Philadelphia was not living in the situation where they could lean back upon a lot of money, power, and prestige. They had little power, and they were small in one sense, but they totally leaned on the power and the ability of God. God's Word became that trumpet to them, and Jesus, the Ultimate Overcomer, opened doors that no man could close. He does the same for every overcomer.

The Feast of Atonement in Relation to The Seven Levels of Promise for the Overcomer

Now, the sixth feast is the Feast of Atonement. Remember that God always establishes the end from the beginning. That is the reason why we can look back in the Old Testament at the seven feasts, and then you can look into the Book of Revelation with the *Seven Levels of Promise for the Overcomer,* that Jesus, had given to the seven churches of Asia Minor, as well as to the churches today. Jesus Himself became the Lamb of God, the sacrifice of atonement that fulfilled the Feast of Atonement for the believers of the seven churches of Asia Minor, and for all of us as well.

The Feast of Tabernacles in Relation to the Seven Levels of Promise for the Overcomer

The seventh feast is the Feast of Tabernacles, and God desires to tabernacle among us. In fact, Jesus said to the church of Laodicea, *"Behold I stand at the door and knock, if any man hear my voice and open the door, I will come in to him, and sup with him, and he with me"* (Rev. 3:20). In addition, Jesus told them, *"To him that overcometh I will grant to sit with Me in My throne, even as I also overcame and sat down with My Father in His throne"* (Revelation 3:21). So, we can see clearly the connection between the Feast of Tabernacles and the words that Jesus spoke to the church of Laodicea.

From this discussion, it should be clear that there is a definite and deliberate correlation with the Feast of Tabernacles when Jesus says, *"Behold I stand at the door and knock."* Jesus wants to come into our innermost being; He wants to tabernacle among us, to dwell in our midst. *"If any man hear My voice and open the door, I will come into him."* Jesus Christ, the Ultimate Overcomer, wants to come in and tabernacle with us in intimate fellowship. Jesus wants to sup with us. Jesus said *"and to him that overcomes I will grant to sit with Me in My throne, even as I also overcame and sat down My Father in His throne"* (Revelation 3:21).

There we have it: the awesome connection between the seven feasts of Israel and the *Seven Levels of Promise for the Overcomer.*

The Seven Feast of Israel In Relation To New Testament Teaching

	One	Two	Three	Four	Five	Six	Seven
	Feast of Passover	Feast of Unleavened Bread	Feast of First Fruits	Feast of Pentecost	Feast of Trumpets	Feast of Atonement	Feast of Tabernacles
	Leviticus 23:5	Leviticus 23:6	Leviticus 23:10	Leviticus 23:15	Leviticus 23:23-25	Leviticus 23:27	Leviticus 23:34
Old Testament	Passover Lamb Slain - Passover points to the Israelites' liberation from slavery in Egypt	The Feast of Unleavened Bread literally speaks of sin being removed from the believer's life	Bring a sheaf of the first fruits of the harvest to the priest to wave before the Lord	The Ingathering 50 days after Passover	The Feast of Trumpets was a two-day feast, symbolizing the fact that no one knows the day or the hour of the Lord's coming.	Yom Kippur was a day of national cleansing for Israel, a time of corporate cleansing in which the high priest would enter the Holy of Holies and sprinkle blood seven times on the mercy seat to atone for the sins of the people.	For seven days the Israelites lived in booths made of leafy branches to commemorate their journey in the wilderness
New Testament	Crucifixion of Jesus Christ, the Lamb slain from the foundation of the world	Burial of Jesus Christ, the Bread of Life, in a borrowed tomb	Resurrection of Jesus Christ, the first fruit of many brethren	Pentecost The Ingathering of 3000 souls–The birth of the church on the Day of Pentecost	Rapture of the Church when the trumpet of God sounds	Tribulation seven year period when the beast, false prophet, and satan, the unholy trinity, will spread their anti-christ message, and God will pour out His wrath	Millennium–The thousand year reign of Jesus Christ, The Ultimate Overcomer
The Seven Churches of Asia Minor mentioned in the Book of Revelation	Ephesus The Loveless Church (Rev. 2:1–7). Lost their love for the Lamb	Smyrna The Suffering Church (Rev. 2:8–11). Faithful unto death	Pergamos The Compromising Church (Rev. 2:12–17). The resurrection of satan's seat–imperial worship	Thyatira The Corrupt Church (Rev. 2:18–29). The ingathering of the Spirit of Jezebel	Sardis The Dead Church (Rev. 3:1–6). "I will come as a thief" because the dead church is not ready	Philadelphia The Faithful Church (Rev. 3:7–13). Kept Christ's word and did not deny His name	Laodicea The Lukewarm Church (Rev. 3:14–22). Only those who overcome will sit with Christ in His throne

Notes For The Overcomer

CHAPTER TEN

The Power to Overcome

The Bible records several accounts of great men of God raising people from the dead. During their lifetimes and ministries Elijah, Elisha, Peter, Paul, and our Lord Jesus Christ Himself, all raised people from the dead as they were anointed of God. A closer look identifies seven of these that are the most prominent.

Seven People Raised From the Dead

In the Bible Besides Jesus

1. Elijah raised the son of the widow at Zarephath from the dead through the power of God (1 Kings 17:17-23).

2. Elisha, who was Elijah's successor, and who received a double portion of Elijah's anointing, raised the son of the Shunammite woman who, after being brought back to life, sneezed seven times (2 Kings 4:32-35).

3. Jesus raised from the dead the only son of the widow of Nain (Luke 7:11-17).

4. Jesus raised from the dead the 12-year-old daughter of Jairus, the ruler of the synagogue (Luke 8:40-56).

5. Jesus raised Lazarus from the dead, after the man had been in the tomb four days (John 11:1-44). After Lazarus stepped forth still wrapped in grave clothes, Jesus said, *"Loose him and let him go."* He says the same thing today: "Loose them and let them go, and let them come to God."

6. Peter raised Tabitha, also known as Dorcas, from the dead

   (Acts 9:36-43).

7. Paul raised Eutychus, who had fallen to his death from a second-floor window late at night while listening to an extended sermon by Paul (Acts 20:9-12).

Seven Details of Creation

1. On the first day God created light. Since He didn't create the sun until the fourth day, it was a Sunday

without a sun, s-u-n, but it was a "Sonday" because the Son was there to give supernatural light.

2. On the second day God separated the land from the water. Likewise, there are things that God wants us to separate from. God is a God of organization. We cannot leave all our clothes on the floor; there are things that need to be put in the closet. Knives and forks that we eat with need to be put away in the drawers in the proper compartments. Leftover food needs to be put into the refrigerator. Our lives need a certain amount of organization, and God originated the concept.

3. On the third day God created the vegetation. The human body, like the earth itself, is made up of 70-percent water, it is important that we eat food with high water content. If 70-percent of our meals, such as fruits and vegetables, was high in water content 30-percent healthy lean meat that was steamed, and accompanied by a beverage that was good for us, such as pure water, natural fruit juice, or tea with no caffeine, we would be taking better care of our bodies and getting back to God's original and natural plan.

4. On the fourth day God created the sun, the moon, and the stars. As we saw before, light already existed. The sun, moon, and stars now gave focal points for the light.

5. On the fifth day, five being the number of grace, God created marine life and birds. Whenever we see fish in the ocean or birds in the air, we need to realize that we are witnessing the grace of God, because these creatures represent His beauty, majesty, and royalty.

6. On the sixth day God created land animals, and, at the end, people. We humans did not evolve from animals; we were just created on the same day. We share a common day, common genetic material, and a common Creator, but that's it. God created all of the land animals, and then He created humankind. Adam's DNA is found in every single human being. Some years ago anthropologists found the bones of a very early woman, and called her "Eve" because the DNA of everyone living was found in her bones. This backs up the Bible's claim that God created humanity. When He created us, He made us of one blood. All the

basic genetic material that was in Adam is present within each one of us.

7. On the seventh day God created the system of rest. A regular cycle of rest is fundamental to life and health. Even Jesus, who was the Son of God, fully God, but also fully man, required regular periods of rest. He made it a practice to get away alone frequently so He could rest and commune with His Father. Jesus was very busy. He healed, He taught, and He preached, but He was never too busy to get away into the mountains to pray, or to pull aside for some "down time." One night, in the midst of a storm, He was down on the hinder part of the boat asleep. Moreover, when they called Him up there, they said, *"Master carest not that we perish?"* What did He say? *"Oh ye of little faith,"* and He rebuked the raging sea, and He spoke to the winds, and He said, *"Peace, be still."* Moreover, God speaks that word, *"Peace, be still"* to each and every one of us today.

The Seven Highest Mountains –

The Overcoming Testimony of Ramon Blanco

Ramon Blanco of Spain holds a unique record: he has climbed the tallest mountain on each continent. What's more, he was seventy years old when he completed this undertaking. We all have summits in our lives, challenges that we face every day. If Mr. Blanco could climb the seven highest mountains, one on each continent, at the age of 70, just imagine what God can do in each one of our lives.

With this remarkable feat of mountain climbing, Ramon Blanco demonstrates the spirit behind *Seven Levels of Promise for the Overcomer*. His determination to climb these mountains on each continent was awesome work that points to the glory and the majesty of our God. Here are the mountains Ramon Blanco climbed, along with their heights and locations. The first seven on the list are collectively referred to as the "seven summits." In addition to these, Mr. Blanco also climbed Mt. Kosciuszko, Australia's tallest peak, and in doing so, succeeded in climbing the tallest mountain on every major landmass on earth.

1. Mount Kilimanjaro, 19,339 feet, Tanzania, Africa
2. Vinson Massif, 16,067 feet, Ellsworth Range, Antarctica

3. Mount Everest, 29,029 feet, Nepal/Tibet, Asia

4. Mount Elbrus, 18,481 feet, Russia, Europe

5. Denali (Mount. McKinley) 20,320 feet, Alaska, North America

6. Aconcagua, 22,840 feet, Argentina, South America

7. Carstenz Pyramid, 16,023 feet, Indonesia, Oceania

8. Mount Kosciuszko, 7,310 feet, Australia.

Few of us could achieve what Ramon Blanco did, but that doesn't matter. You may not be 70 years old, but you've got seven days in the week. Just take life one day at a time, and trust God. First, set aside one day especially for rest and worship. We need both every day, but we also need one day a week to put our special touch and a highlight on it. We can worship at work. We can worship on the street. We can worship at home. We can worship anywhere. Worship the Lord in spirit and in truth. We need to lay aside some time and get that strength for the journey, because there are some summits that God has in our lives. There are some high mountains in our lives. I know there are some mountains that need to be moved, but there are others that we have to learn to say, like Caleb of old, *"Give me this mountain."*

Caleb had to go up into those mountains and kill the giants, and we have to go up into the seven summits, the seven mountains in our lives and do the same. We have to go into the mountain of education and slay the giants that are trying to mis-educate our children, and to rape our children educationally. We have to go and slay those giants in these seven summits, these highest mountains that influence our community. We have to go up on the summit, the highest mountain of politics, and let our politicians realize that there is trouble in our communities. We have to come together. We have to pray together. We have to network together and coordinate the skill, and the talent, and the ability that we have received. We have to harness it all for the betterment, enrichment, and enhancement of our communities spiritually, socially, and economically. We must all bind together and encourage each other to stop being consumers all the time.

In the African-American community we spend more than many nations spend. We just consume and buy different goods that depreciate. We all need to make investments within our homes, our families, and our communities that will strengthen and build them up. We need to begin now to look at those things that will move us forward. We have to look at the summits, the highest mountains of entertainment. Let our entertainers, our athletes, and those in music and all different types of fields know that we need them to invest back into our communities. There are youth centers that they can invest in, where people have been faithfully coming every day, working with our children, keeping them off the street, and off of drugs. Our challenge is to convince our entertainers and sports figures not to abandon the churches or the voice of God, and not to have the spirit of Jezebel, but a spirit that is sensitive to God. Instead of being part of the system, or the synagogue of Satan, or caught up in the seat of Satan in worldly corrupt systems, they need to get involved with the system that gives back and that pours into our communities.

We know that things can be turned around. We have to go up into these high mountains and prevail. We have to deal with the public relations and get out into the community. Realize that you must get involved. We know that you are hurting, that you are suffering. There is a level of leadership that comes from the pew. There is a level of leadership that comes from the ghetto. There is a level of leadership that comes from community involvement and the connection between the pulpit and the pew.

There is an undeniable connection between the leaders within the seats of government and the people they represent, and that connection is key. It represents one of these summits that we must climb. We have to conquer the issues that are out there each day. We have to take back all of these different fields. We have to deal with the arts and realize that there is a ministry of the arts. Not only must the sports figures get involved, but also the arts have to be seen as worship to God, whether it is dance, music, or the spoken word. We must give the arts back to the Lord. Bring the art centers back into the heart of the community, so that the members of the community can come out to hear our children sing and speak. Children and youth receiving and performing small parts in plays and programs at church school, public school, or youth center is the beginning of raising up leaders through the various disciplines such as the arts. Through the arts, souls and lives can be totally transformed. They can be changed, and then the mountain or the summit is moving from mere mundane religion to a truly passionate relationship with Jesus Christ, the Ultimate Overcomer.

Yes, we have to deal with the arts, but we also have to deal with sports. We have to deal with politics. We have to deal with the community. We have to deal with the economics. We have to deal with each of these things, but most of all, we have to move from dull and mundane religion. There are many good things that religion does for many different people, but Jesus said, "You must be born again."

No matter how much prestige, dignity, or community religion brings, it cannot get us into Heaven. Only the blood of Jesus can do that. Therefore, we need to recognize that spiritually there are seven summits also. Spiritually there are seven high mountains, and we've got to deal with each and every one of them spiritually, socially, politically, economically, and in every area of life.

Seven Significant Relationship Stages or Experiences of Life

There are seven significant relationships or relationship stages in everyday life. When we talk about *Seven Levels of*

Promise for the Overcomer, they apply also to these **seven significant relationship stages of life.**

1. Single
2. Engaged
3. Married
4. Separated
5. Divorced
6. Remarried
7. Widowed

In Matthew 19:3-11, Jesus tackles the hard issues of relationships such engagement, marriage, divorce, and remarriage. Jesus pulls no punches, but He is more than fair in each case.

✝ **Matthew 19:3-12:**

"The Pharisees also came unto him, tempting him, and saying unto him, Is it lawful for a man to put away his wife for every cause? And he answered and said unto them, Have ye not read, that he which made them at the beginning made them male and female, And said, For this cause shall a man leave father and mother, and shall cleave to his wife: and

they twain shall be one flesh? Wherefore they are no more twain, but one flesh. What therefore God hath joined together, let not man put asunder. They say unto him, Why did Moses then command to give a writing of divorcement, and to put her away? He saith unto them, Moses because of the hardness of your hearts suffered you to put away your wives: but from the beginning it was not so. And I say unto you, Whosoever shall put away his wife, except it be for fornication, and shall marry another, committeth adultery: and whoso marrieth her which is put away doth commit adultery. His disciples say unto him, If the case of the man be so with his wife, it is not good to marry. But he said unto them, All men cannot receive this saying, save they to whom it is given. For there are some eunuchs, which were so born from their mother's womb: and there are some eunuchs, which were made eunuchs of men: and there be eunuchs, which have made themselves eunuchs for the kingdom of heaven's sake. He that is able to receive it, let him receive it."

1.) Ministry to Singles

The key thing in terms of being single is to be whole in your own innermost being. If a single person who is whole gets together with another single person who is whole, the result is a whole couple. However, if two people get together who are not whole, or one person is whole and the other is not, the result will be a couple that are *"unequally yoked"*, which will be a real nightmare.

It is important to be whole as a single; to find and rekindle your romance with your first love, because you do not want to be single and hurt in the second death. There are many pressures to deal with being single. Some singles have children from another relationship and face the challenge of learning how to live their life to the fullest. They want the knowledge and assurance that in the next level of this life, in their relationship with Jesus Christ, they will be with Him for eternity, both now and forever. They want to know that they will not be hurt in the second death, because they have been hurt, battered, broken, and bruised already in too many earthly relationships. There have been losses. There have been those frauds who call themselves friends, and lovers who did them in or dogged them out. When you are single, you want to have a singleness of mind. You want to have a true positive focus that says, "I am going to live for the Lord. I am going back to school to further my education. I am going to get my life back on track. I am going to be an ambassador for Jesus Christ. I am going to be that brother or sister, that servant, that friend for my friend that sticks closer than a brother."

2.) Ministry to Engaged Couples

In Bible days, there were three basic steps that the Jews took before marriage. First of all, both families had to come to complete agreement concerning the union. Second, an announcement was made to the general community. Third, the man and women were betrothed, or what we would call in today's society engaged. After a period of betrothal that usually lasted one year, during which time the couple was considered married, but did not live together, the formal wedding service was observed with great joy and celebration. Only then did the couple begin to live together as husband and wife and consummate the marriage union. Biblical and historical betrothal was similar in nature to what we call engagement today, except that our society does not honor the seriousness of engagement as in Bible days. When a Jewish couple was betrothed during Bible times, they were already bound together by a fully legal contract that could only be broken through the pains of death or divorce.

Any Christian couple who is seriously considering marriage needs to realize the total depth of this type of commitment, and not jump into it lightly. There is an African proverb which states: "A man without a wife is like a vase without flowers." Therefore engagement is the necessary process which teaches a couple how not to break the vase or end up killing the flowers that the marital relationship represents. God intends the marriage union to be a lifelong commitment, not a temporary agreement or short-lived arrangement. The Bible states this about marriage: *"'This explains why a man leaves his father and mother and is joined to his wife, and the two are united into one.' Since they are no longer two but one, let no one separate them, for God has joined them together"* (Mark 10:7-9, NLT).

Christians need to make sure they have a clear understanding of the personality and the temperament of the person they may marry long before becoming engaged. It is important to find out what your potential mate is like when they are angry. Are they a mental, physical, or verbal abuser? Spousal abuse can be avoided in many cases if one discovers their potential mates' worst reactions to anger early on in the relationship. If your date and potential mate practices mental, physical, or verbal abuse on you prior to engagement or marriage then wait for a new mate who will truly love you and respect you. If they slam you against the wall, call you no good and ugly prior to or even during the engagement that is a clear sign that the abuse would only get worst during marriage. The Bible says that Christians cannot team up with and live in harmony with unbelievers (2 Corinthians 6:14-15). Such an unequal yoking almost guarantees that the Christian will be pulled away from Christ because, as the Bible says, "'Bad company corrupts good character'" (1 Corinthians 15:33). The only way to have a God-honoring, stable foundation for a marriage is to be firmly grounded in one's faith, and make sure that the potential partner is equally dedicated to God.

All of us as believers should live our lives with God in the driver's seat, so to speak. He wants to be a part of every aspect of our lives, including whom we marry. Having a clear understanding of God's Word, developing a personal relationship with Him through prayer, and yielding to the direction of the Holy Spirit are the most important steps in determining His will for us. The world's advice on dating and engagement should only be considered in light of God's eternal truths in Scripture. If we seek His will in all we do, He will direct our paths (Proverbs 3:5-6).

3.) Ministry to Married Couples

✝ Matthew 19:4-6:

"And he answered and said unto them, Have ye not read, that he which made them at the beginning made them male and female, And said, For this cause shall a man leave father and mother, and shall cleave to his wife: and they twain shall be one flesh? Wherefore they are no more twain, but one flesh. What therefore God hath joined together, let not man put asunder."

Marriage is the third significant relationship status of life. When you are married, you do not want to be in a place similar to that of the church of Pergamos, where Satan's seat was. Work to keep your marriage fresh and your romance alive. Don't stop dating just because you are married. One of the best ways to keep the romance alive in your marriage is for you and your mate to go out together regularly. You don't want to lose that first love, because that normally leads to separation. Make it special. Cook your mate his or her favorite meal. Give your mate a massage. Take time to keep the fire burning. Learn to laugh. Learn repeatedly to love your mate. You do not want Satan's seat to be in your marriage. Learn together to flow in the *Seven Levels of Promise for the Overcomer*. Seek after the "hidden manna." We all need that hidden manna in our lives. We need that bread from above that only God can provide. We need Jesus Christ to bring some fresh bread into our lives and marriages to renew and refresh the relationship. We need Jesus to bring guidance, hope, and healing to that relationship, so that our marriage will last and stand the test of time.

✟ **Ephesians 5:23:**

"For the husband is the head of the wife, even as Christ is the head of the church: and he is the saviour of the body."

✟ **Ephesians 5:33:**

"Nevertheless let every one of you in particular so love his wife even as himself; and the wife see that she reverence her husband."

4.) Ministry to the Separated

In the seven significant relationships and status in life, there are times when people become separated—even married people. Separation can exist without divorce (which is the next step). Sometimes people can be separated and live in the same house. They can share the same room and even the same bed and still be separated. This is similar to the situation that existed in the church of Thyatira. They loved God, yet tolerated the spirit of Jezebel. They were separated, they were disconnected, and the spirit of Jezebel got in and seduced the servants of God into fornication and eating foods that had been sacrificed to idols. They had gotten into the depths of Satan; they were separated from Jesus Christ.

Disconnection can get us totally out of the power zone from God. Distractions can cause disconnections, which can result in separation. God is there, but His weighty presence may not be felt. We do not want to get to that point. Therefore, we have to look closely at what happened in the church of Thyatira, so we do not allow ourselves to get caught up in the depths of Satan and in the spirit of Jezebel.

When separation occurs, it is always accompanied by deep hurt and pain. If you have become separated, the pain of that separation must be healed before you can be made whole. If you turn to Christ for help, you will not remain battered, broken, and bruised. There is inner healing and essential wholeness for you. If you trust God, you can overcome in the midst of it. Remember those stirring words, "Deep in my heart I do believe that we shall overcome."

People who are separated sometimes get back together. These folks have learned that God heals marriages. It does not always happen that way, but God can do it. No matter what your situation is, be sensitive to what God desires to do in the midst of it. Getting back together and rebuilding the relationship will require a lot of work. The couple will have to agree to work together, respect each other, and be civil with each other. This is not a time to get in each other's face. That spirit of Jezebel can get mighty nasty in men, as well as in women, because the spirit of Jezebel wants to seduce the saints into harmful situations. The spirit of Jezebel wants to cut off the heads of the prophets.

Even separated people can become overcomers. Separation does not automatically disqualify you. Even if you have been separated, you can still have the power over the nations; you can rule with a rod of iron, and God can break up some situations. When Jesus Christ breaks up some situations, like pottery that has been broken up into little pieces, those little pieces can represent souls that can be brought into the kingdom through your personal testimony of being battered, broken, and bruised. Always remember that the Book of Revelation declares that we overcome Satan by the blood of the Lamb, and the word of our testimony. My brothers, my sister, plead the blood of Jesus, and testify of the goodness of the Lord. Jesus can wet down the broken pieces and remold you again. Put yourself in the hand of the Potter, and even in the midst of your separation, Jesus can remold you into a whole new vessel.

5.) Ministry to the Divorced

God the Father hates divorce. Therefore, Jesus hates divorce. Jesus' statement concerning divorce is the strongest statement against divorce in the New Testament. Yet Jesus ends His teaching on divorce by saying, *"All men cannot receive this saying,"* which essentially does the same thing that the Law of Moses did. Open the door of possibility for divorce with the harsh warning that God hates it. When reading these verses from Matthew, a divorced brother or sister in Christ must find comfort in the truth that these statements were made before Jesus died on the cross for our sins. Jesus still hates divorce, but there is grace, and ultimate empowerment to fulfill God's law, for the truly repentant, abused, and wounded heart and soul.

✝ **Matthew 19:7-11:**

"They say unto him, Why did Moses then command to give a writing of divorcement, and to put her away? He saith unto them, Moses because of the hardness of your hearts suffered you to put away your wives: but from the beginning it was not so. And I say unto you, Whosoever shall put away his wife, except it be for fornication, and shall marry another, committeth adultery: and whoso marrieth her which is put away doth commit adultery. His disciples say unto him, If the case of the man be so with his wife, it is not good to marry. But he said unto them, All men cannot receive this saying, save they to whom it is given."

Jesus hits divorce hard with a Scriptural sledgehammer, but admittedly, our Savior also clearly shows great compassion for the divorced. Many people ignore this portion of the well-known text. Jesus admits that not everyone can receive this saying. So we must be careful never to use this scripture to judge anyone at all, because we will instantly take it out of context. If Jesus, the ultimate Overcomer, dealt with divorce with both utterly firm strength and complete godly compassion for the divorced sister or brother, then we must never misuse His very words to belittle a divorced brother or sister who has already been devastated by the experience.

Divorced brothers and sisters are also called to be overcomers. Always remember that God knows first hand what it is like for Israel to cheat, sleep, and fool around on the Lover of their souls in the Old Testament. Then, in the New Testament, the Christian church washed in Jesus Christ's very own blood loses her first love, or gets into the seat of Satan. Even a casual reading of Revelation chapters two and three makes it clear that Jesus Christ understands the plight of the divorced. God absolutely hates divorce, but He also clearly understands it from painful personal experiences from the dawn of time right up to this very moment.

At the same time, we must be careful never to use this portion of the book to justify divorce. Jesus ministered to the woman at the well who had six husbands, and became the seventh man in her life, the only one who could truly liberate her both within and without. If we truly believe in kingdom ministry, which simply means service, we must never run away from the harsh sayings of Jesus Christ. We must read the whole Scripture, with the verses above and below, and not take it out of context.

To the brother or sister who has been divorced, let me say this: you can still become an overcomer. God can give you power over the nations. He can allow you to come forth with the power to speak into people's lives, but only if you allow Him to make you an overcomer.

6.) Ministry to the Remarried

Remarriage is the sixth stage of relationships in life. People remarry after either divorce or widowhood, but not everyone who becomes "single again" chooses to remarry.

My mother served as a pastor's wife for thirty-five years at Mt. Sinai Baptist Church where I now serve as pastor. For over forty years my mother served as a minister's wife, first as the wife of the assistant pastor, my father, before he became pastor.

My father and mother always said, "Till death do us part," and many years after he had passed away, my mother remarried, to Bishop Arthur Hull from New Jersey. Now the Lord is blessing her; the Lord is using her in an awesome manner.

Most people do not have a problem when a person who is widowed remarries. But plenty of folk have major problems when a divorced person with a former spouse who is still alive gets married. Their righteous anger stems from Jesus' remarks made in Matthew chapter nineteen. Yet it is extremely important to read every single word that Jesus said concerning marriage, divorce, and remarriage, because He pulls no punches at all.

After saying that all men could not receive His saying regarding divorce, but only those to whom it was given, Jesus concluded, *"For there are some eunuchs, which were so born from their mother's womb: and there are some eunuchs, which were made eunuchs of men: and there be eunuchs, which have made themselves eunuchs for the kingdom of heaven's sake. He that is able to receive it, let him receive it"* (Matthew 19:12). If we properly studied the Scriptures concerning the hard issues of life such as marriage, divorce, and remarriage, we would have more healthy relationships, for the fresh revelation of eternal truth for relationships would put the fear and reverence of God back in the house.

Within the parameters of these seven life stages, there are many types of committed relationships that don't fall precisely into any of these categories. Committed relationships can take many different forms depending on the circumstances. A committed relationship could be a grandmother and a grandson, where the father and mother are not around, but the grandmother is there, and she takes care of that grandson. It could be two homeless people who watch out for each other. They may live in an alley, but they are committed to each other. It could be a husband and a wife, a brother and sister, but it is a committed relationship. This topic of committed relationships is very broad and covers many different types of relationships.

It could be a person who is up in age and lives in a nursing home, and a nurse who has bonded with that person, and who really cares for that person. This concept of committed relationships is very broad in scope. It carries the reward of each person being there for the other and being supportive of each other.

7.) Ministry to The Widow

The seventh and last significant relationship status in life is that of being widowed. Some widowed persons, like my mother, choose to remarry, but others do not. Widowhood has made them single again, but it is a different level of singleness. God says in His Word that He would bring justice to the widow. When we look at this, and then we look at the church of Laodicea, we see how the Lord said that He stands at the door and knocks, and if any of us hears His voice and opens the door, He will come in and dwell with us. Christ understands what it is to be lonely, but not alone. We can be lonely yet not be alone, because the Lord is always with us.

Seven Places People Reside

1. Homeless—Outside on the street, in an alley, or even in a homeless shelter.

2. A house—big or small, or even a mobile home.

3. A hotel.

4. A room.

5. An apartment.

6. A condominium or townhouse.

7. A full-fledged mansion,

These are the seven places people reside. Some people are homeless. In New York City, you can go to the Bowery, or any number of different places, and find people who live in boxes. There are people who construct makeshift homes outside, and even though it may be freezing, they find a way to get warm. Even though they are living outside, and may have lived out there for years, they have survived. Most homeless spend some time periodically in homeless shelters, which are part of their homeless situation, but provides no permanent home.

Then there is the house that somebody rents, or perhaps owns, and lives there alone, or with a family.

Some people who are rich and affluent live in hotels, because they love the service they receive. They split their time between classy hotels in New York and Hong Kong and all other major cities of the world.

At the other end of the spectrum are those who are struggling and robbing Peter to pay Paul and living out of cheap hotels, dingy dives that they pay for by the week from the income they receive from little jobs they find here and there. These "kings of the road" go from city to city, and from town to town, taking whatever odd jobs they can find.

There are also those who live in a single room, whether in a house, a hotel, or an apartment, that they pay for by the week or month. Sometimes, depending on the situation, the room may have been donated to them.

I remember living in Hempstead for a period of time, and a family member reached out to us and embraced us. My father was dying of cancer, my wife was pregnant with our third child, and there we were in Hempstead in one room, because somebody believed in us, had faith in us, and helped us out. We were there in that one room: me, Brenda, Yolanda, Jordan, and Faith, who had not yet been born. At that time we were working on getting our first home. I also had just become pastor of Mt. Sinai Baptist Church Cathedral. So I had several significant things really, when I totaled them up I had about seven significant things going on all at one time.

So when I talk about *Seven Levels of Promise for the Overcomer* believe me I had some things I had to overcome. Some things I had to deal with, some pressures, some ups and downs I was going through, but yet through those times God spoke in that room, God ministered in that room, and He brought us through. He brought us together as a family, and we will never forget those precious times.

Seven Basic Tips for Achieving Debt Reduction –

One thing we need to remember as we strive to become overcomers is the negative nature and system of Satan that desires to bring people to the point where they cannot buy or sell without total submission to his evil influence. Economic oppression of the masses, priority deception of the wealthy, slavery, deep poverty, and the teaching in context of Revelation 13:16-18 all point to this eternal truth.

✝ **Revelation 13:16-18:**

"And he causeth all, both small and great, rich and poor, free and bond, to receive a mark in their right hand, or in their foreheads: And that no man might buy or sell, save he

that had the mark, or the name of the beast, or the number of his name. Here is wisdom. Let him that hath understanding count the number of the beast: for it is the number of a man; and his number is Six hundred threescore and six. "

Take action now! Begin systematically to pay off your debts so you can be a blessing in the advancement of the Kingdom of God. Do not be controlled by negative debt, the system of the mark of the beast now, or in the literal future that Revelation 13:16-18 clearly speaks of. No matter what your social/economic status is, let the seal of God, and not the mark of the beast, make the difference in your life. Consider these seven tips for getting out of debt.

1) Total Commitment to Change.

First, you must be totally committed to changing your past and current negative spending habits and all bad financial patterns. You must also choose to spend less money than you make, no matter how tempting the higher-class life may be to you. This is a beneficial practice for all, but this principle is especially important and crucial to those who are in debt. Total commitment is important. It is like the humorous story of the hungry chicken and pig. In the story, the chicken said, "I will give eggs if you give ham". The pig instantly responded and said "for you to give eggs is fairly easy, but for me to give ham requires total commitment". Achieving and maintaining debt reduction requires total commitment.

2) Cut Up and Cut Back On Credit Card Overspending

One way to make sure that you do not overspend is to cut up those credit cards and spend only the cash that you have on hand. This will ensure that you are only spending what you have the means to spend. Remember to continue to keep track of your spending, though, and spend it wisely. Even if cash is more controllable, you do not want to spend all of your cash at the mall and come to find there is nothing left when you get to the food market.

3) Keep Track of All of Your Spending.

Do you know how you got into debt in the first place? Have you looked at why you do not seem to be getting out? Knowledge is crucial to changing your habits. Keeping track of all monies coming in and going out will allow you to see where the money is going, and where you could make changes to better control your money.

4) Find Out Your Worst Debts And Attack Them First.

Debts on items that can appreciate and have tax advantages are the least risky. A home is the best example of this, school loans could also fall into this category. Years down the road, you are most likely to have increased the value of that purchase. Debts on items that come and go are the worst, because once the money is gone, you are left with nothing. In addition, a general rule of thumb is that anything with an interest rate over 10% is going to hurt. Credit card lovers be warned!

5) Go After A Better Rate

You can usually find a lender willing to consolidate your debt for a better rate, which will make payments more manageable. This is because lenders love to make money off you and the more you owe, the more they get. Keeping this in mind, take advantage of their greed. Call up your credit card companies and tell them that you would love to stay with them but you have received many offers from other companies that are willing to give you a lower rate. If you are persistent, you are likely to get a break. If they refuse and you do find a better rate, take your business elsewhere!

6) Make A Payment Plan.

Do it yourself or hire a financial advisor to help. There are also many inexpensive software programs that can help you identify your debt and create a payment plan. Manipulate the numbers to see how much quicker your debt will be paid off if you make larger payments now. This can be just the encouraging boost you need to be focused.

7) Take a Stand for Your Financial Integrity and Future

Once you have resolved to pay off your debt, stay strong, and be pleased with yourself for the decision you have made. The harder you work in the beginning, the sooner you will be paid off. Do not lose track of your goals. The end may appear far off, but you will get there! Again, let me reiterate that no matter what your social/economic status is, let the seal of God and not the mark of the beast make the difference in your life.

You were born to be an overcomer. You can overcome your economic past and present, and have a sound future full of financial integrity.

Seven More Scriptures Concerning the Mark of the Beast in the Future

1) Revelation 13:16

*"And he causeth all, both small and great, rich and poor, free and bond, to receive a **mark** in their right hand, or in their foreheads:"*

2) Revelation 13:17:

*"And that no man might buy or sell, save he that had the **mark**, or the name of the beast, or the number of his name."*

3) Revelation 14:9:

*"And the third angel followed them, saying with a loud voice, If any man worship the beast and his image, and receive his **mark** in his forehead, or in his hand,"*

4) Revelation 14:11:

*"And the smoke of their torment ascendeth up forever and ever: and they have no rest day nor night, who worship the beast and his image, and whosoever receiveth the **mark** of his name."*

5) Revelation 15:2:

*"And I saw as it were a sea of glass mingled with fire: and them that had gotten the victory over the beast, and over his image, and over his **mark**, and over the number of his name, stand on the sea of glass, having the harps of God."*

6) Revelation 16:2:

*"And the first went, and poured out his vial upon the earth; and there fell a noisome and grievous sore upon the men which had the **mark** of the beast, and upon them which worshipped his image."*

7) Revelation 19:20:

*"And the beast was taken, and with him the false prophet that wrought miracles before him, with which he deceived them that had received the **mark** of the beast, and them that*

worshipped his image. These both were cast alive into a lake of fire burning with brimstone."

No matter what your social/economic status is, let the Word of God, the Sevenfold Spirit of God, and the seal of God, and not the mark of the beast, make the difference in your life. Do business God's way. Occupy until Jesus comes. Do business until Jesus comes. Take action now. Advance the Kingdom of God on earth. *"Even so, come Lord Jesus."*

Embrace the Grace – The Power to Overcome

It is extremely interesting to realize that the Book of Revelation, which is widely associated with God's wrathful judgment (the Seven Seals, the Seven Trumpets, Seven Vials of Wrath and etc.), begins in Revelation 1:4 and ends Revelation 22:21 with the timely subject of God's grace.

Dietrich Bonhoeffer

The 39 year-old German theologian and Lutheran pastor, Dietrich Bonhoeffer, was brutally executed (hanged to death) for plotting against the mass murder of Jews in concentration camps by German leader - Adolf Hilter. Pastor Bonhoeffer's theology promoted "religionless Christianity" and the true enhance of grace, long before the present day emphasis on "it's not about religion but relationship" that ministers to the battered, broken, and bruised to make them whole. Pastor Bonhoeffer was a "religionless Christian" overcomer and martyr who lost his life for standing against pure evil, as expressed in the highly abusive and oppressive dictatorship of Hitler. Pastor Bonhoeffer truly embraced grace when he wrote that "Cheap grace is grace without discipleship, grace without the cross, grace without Jesus Christ, living and incarnate."[49] Bonhoeffer chose discipleship over dictatorship, and embraced

---

[49] Dietrich Bonhoeffer, German Theologian and Lutheran Pastor, The Cost of Discipleship, 1937

grace and opposed Hilter's gruesome anti-christ acts of evil against Jews.

If the prophetic Book of Revelation begins and ends with the grace of God, then we Christians, who are the "people of the Way," should begin and end the same way. The Book of Revelation clearly sends the message that if we do not embrace the true grace of God, then we will experience the true judgment of God. Embrace the grace, the power to endure, the power to overcome the obstacles of life.

1) Revelation 1:4-5:

"John to the seven churches which are in Asia: Grace be unto you, and peace, from him which is, and which was, and which is to come; and from the seven Spirits which are before his throne; And from Jesus Christ, who is the faithful witness, and the first begotten of the dead, and the prince of the kings of the earth. Unto him that loved us, and washed us from our sins in his own blood."

2) Revelation 22:21:

"The grace of our Lord Jesus Christ be with you all. Amen."

Noted author Stormie Omartian, in her book entitled, *Seven Prayers That Will Change Your Life Forever,* defines seven important types of prayer. They are as follows:

1. The Prayer of Confession
2. The Prayer of Salvation
3. The Prayer of Release
4. The Prayer of Submission
5. The Prayer of Praise
6. The Prayer of Promise
7. The Prayer of Blessing

Mrs. Omartian states, "Without prayer, the full purpose God has for you can't happen."[50]

---

[50] Stormie Omartian, *Seven Prayers That Will Change Your Life Forever,* (Nashville: J.Countryman, a division of Thomas Nelson, Inc., 2006), 12.

Giana

My four year-old niece's name, Giana, means, "God's grace." Precious little Giana has certainly experienced God's amazing grace. When she was born, she was in dire need of a liver transplant. Before the age of two, little Giana received a new liver in Cleveland, Ohio. To date, Giana has had nearly twenty different surgeries and various other procedures. By God's grace, Giana is a true overcomer. She has to take anti-rejection medicine every day, and by God's awesome grace, Giana's body has not rejected her liver. It was amazing to actually see a precious little three year-old girl take her own various liver medicines, one by one, by mouth, under her mother's care and supervision. May the grace of the Lord Jesus, which has certainly been with our little Giana, be with all God's people.

**Embrace the grace,
the power to endure, and the power to
overcome.
The revelation is relevant.**

Notes For The Overcomer

EPILOGUE

Seven Elements and Principles of

Art in the Book of Revelation

Just as the Book of Revelation is literally outlined in sevens, there are also seven elements of art and seven principles of art in the academic world. God, the greatest Educator, Himself uses all of the seven elements of art and seven principles of art with great distinction to paint a vivid picture of the end times in the Book of Revelation.

The seven elements of art are the components used to create, or build a work of art. They are: Line, Shape, Form, Value, Texture, Color, Space.

1) Line is a mark or hash mark made on a surface.

✝ **Revelation 13:16:**

*"And he causeth all, both small and great, rich and poor, free and bond, to receive a **mark** in their right hand, or in their foreheads."*

2) Shape has two dimensions, length and width, and is represented as an enclosed area defined by line, color, value, texture, space, or form.

✝ **Revelation 9:7:**

*"And the **shapes** of the locusts were like unto horses prepared unto battle; and on their heads were as it were crowns like gold, and their faces were as the faces of men."*

3) Form appears three dimensional and encloses volume. Form has three dimensions, an artistic trinity: length, width, and height (cube, sphere, pyramid, and cylinder).

✝ **Revelation 21:16:**

*"And the city lieth **foursquare**, and the length is as large as the breadth: and he measured the city with the reed, twelve thousand furlongs. **The length and the breadth and the height of it are equal.**"*

4) Value refers to changes of a base color, and includes light, medium, and dark areas. Value is determined by how much light a surface reflects or absorbs. Highlights, midtones, shadows, and cast shadows may all show up as different intensities of the same color.

✝ **Revelation 21:21:**

*"And the twelve gates were twelve pearls: every several gate was of one pearl: and the street of the city was **pure gold, as it were transparent glass.**"*

5) **Texture** is the tactile quality of a surface or its representation, what a surface appears to feel like. The three basic types of texture are *actual, simulated,* and *invented* texture.

✝ **Revelation 1:14:**

*"His head and his hairs were white like **wool**, as white as snow; and his eyes were as a flame of fire."*

6) **Color** is derived from reflected light. The sensation of color is aroused in the brain by response of the eyes to different wavelengths of light. A color has three parts: hue (color name), intensity (strength/purity), and value (lightness and darkness).

✝ **Revelation 1:15:**

*"And his feet like unto **fine brass**, as if they burned in a furnace; and his voice as the sound of many waters."*

✝ **Revelation 4:3-4:**

*"And he that sat was to look upon like a jasper and a sardine stone: and there was a **rainbow** round about the throne, in sight like unto an **emerald**. And round about the throne were four and twenty seats: and upon the seats I saw four and twenty elders sitting, clothed in **white** raiment; and they had on their heads crowns of **gold**."*

7) **Space** is the creation of visual perspective, and the illusion of depth; the distance around, between, above, below, and within an object or group of objects.

✝ **Revelation 14:20:**

*"And the winepress was trodden without the city, and blood came out of the winepress, even unto the horse bridles, by the **space** of a thousand and six hundred furlongs."*

✝ **Revelation 17:10:**

*"And there are seven kings: five are fallen, and one is, and the other is not yet come; and when he cometh, he must continue a short **space**."*

The Seven Principles of Art:

Balance, Focal Point, Gradation, Movement, Proportion, Rhythm, and Variety

The seven principles of art define the way the elements of art are organized, or arranged, in a work of art.

1) Balance or **Visual Weight** is the element arranged to create a sense of stability.

✝ **Revelation 6:5:**

"And when he had opened the third seal, I heard the third beast say, Come and see. And I beheld, and lo a black horse; and he that sat on him had a pair of balances in his hand."

2) Focal Point or **Area of Emphasis** combines elements to point out their differences. The area of greatest difference gets our attention.

✝ **Revelation 21:1:**

*"And I saw a **new heaven** and a **new** earth: for the first **heaven** and the first earth were passed away; and there was no more sea."*

3) Gradation occurs when elements are combined using a series of gradual changes.

✝ **Revelation 8:1:**

"And when he had opened the seventh seal, there was silence in heaven about the space of half an hour."

4) Movement is how the viewer's eye moves throughout the work of art. Some artists combine elements to create the illusion of action; others create a sense of perspective and space. The Book of Revelation is no illusion. Its movement utilizes perspective and space effectively for a high impact action scene that the reader will never forget.

✝ **Revelation 8:2-5:**

*"And I saw the seven angels which stood before God; and to them were given seven trumpets. And another angel came and stood at the altar, having a golden censer; and there was given unto him much incense, that he should offer it with the prayers of all saints upon the golden altar which was before the throne. And the smoke of the incense, which came with the prayers of the saints, ascended up before God out of the angel's hand. And the angel took the censer, and **filled it with fire of the altar,** and **cast it into the earth: and there were voices, and thunderings, and lightnings, and an earthquake.**"*

5) Proportion occurs when elements are combined to create size relationships.

✝ **Revelation 21:16-17:**

"And the city lieth foursquare, and the length is as large as the breadth: and he measured the city with the reed, twelve thousand furlongs. The length and the breadth and the height of it are equal. And he measured the wall thereof, an hundred and forty and four cubits, according to the measure of a man, that is, of the angel."

6) **Rhythm** occurs when elements are repeated to create a visual tempo. Our eye moves throughout the piece gathering similar elements. Rhythm creates visual unity; it is what holds the work together. The sevenfold usage of the word **overcometh** in Revelation chapters two and three are a classic example of divinely artistic rhythm found so richly in the Book of Revelation.

✟ **Revelation 2:7:**

> *"He that hath an ear, let him hear what the Spirit saith unto the churches; To him that **overcometh** will I give to eat of the tree of life, which is in the midst of the paradise of God."*

✟ **Revelation 2:11:**

> *"He that hath an ear, let him hear what the Spirit saith unto the churches; He that **overcometh** shall not be hurt of the second death."*

✟ **Revelation 2:17:**

> *"He that hath an ear, let him hear what the Spirit saith unto the churches; To him that **overcometh** will I give to eat of the hidden manna, and will give him a white stone, and in the stone a new name written, which no man knoweth saving he that receiveth it."*

✟ **Revelation 2:26:**

*"And he that **overcometh**, and keepeth my works unto the end, to him will I give power over the nations."*

✟ **Revelation 3:5:**

*"He that **overcometh**, the same shall be clothed in white raiment; and I will not blot out his name out of the book of life, but I will confess his name before my Father, and before his angels."*

✟ **Revelation 3:12:**

*"Him that **overcometh** will I make a pillar in the temple of my God, and he shall go no more out: and I will write upon him the name of my God, and the name of the city of my God, which is new Jerusalem, which cometh down out of heaven from my God: and I will write upon him my new name."*

✟ **Revelation 3:21:**

*"To him that **overcometh** will I grant to sit with me in my throne, even as I also overcame, and am set down with my Father in his throne."*

7) **Variety** involves combining contrasting elements, such as good and evil, to create visual interest. These are the parts of the image that stand out to establish a figure ground relationship, the subject and a background. The vividly detailed and action-packed drama of the evil beast and the

fallen kings of the earth, and their failed attempt to defeat Jesus Christ, and His army of blood-washed believers, is a wonderful example of God-given artistic variety found in the Book of Revelation. In no way, shape, or form does the Seven Elements and Principles of Art found in the Book of Revelation take away from the rock-solid truth that the prophetic events of Revelation will actually occur as stated in the ancient text.

✟ **Revelation 17:14:**

*"These shall make war with the Lamb, and **the Lamb shall overcome them**: for he is Lord of lords, and King of kings: **and they that are with him are called, and chosen, and faithful.**"*

✟ **Revelation 19:19-21:**

"And I saw the beast, and the kings of the earth, and their armies, gathered together to make war against him that sat on the horse, and against his army. And the beast was taken, and with him the false prophet that wrought miracles before him, with which he deceived them that had received the mark of the beast, and them that worshipped his image. These both were cast alive into a lake of fire burning with brimstone. And the remnant were slain with the sword of him that sat upon the horse, which sword proceeded out of his mouth: and all the fowls were filled with their flesh."

**No matter what
you are going through—
testing, trials, or
tribulation—
stay with Jesus,
the ultimate Overcomer,
for in the end, *we win*!**

NOTES

1) Glenn Usry & Craig S. Keener, Black Man's Religion – Can Christianity Be Afrocentric?, Inter Varsity Press, Downers Grove, Illinois, pg. 110

2) Rosa Parks, The Mother of the Civil Rights Movement, concerning preparing our children to overcome.

3) Rev. Dr. Martin Luther King, Jr., Speaking against lynchings, Cornell College, Mount Vernon, Iowa. Reported in the Wall Street Journal, November 13, 1962

4) Letter From Birmingham Jail, Rev. Dr. Martin Luther King, Jr., April 16, 1963, The Estate of Martin Luther King, Jr.

5) Rev. Dr. Martin Luther King, Jr., March on Washington Speech, Lincoln Memorial, Washington, D.C., August 28, 1963

6) Lisa Miller, "Religion: Revelation Revealed - Beyond Fear: The Bible's last book is both terrifying and beautiful. But it ends with a message of hope." *Newsweek*, May 24, 2007

7) Ibid; Miller, *Newsweek*

8) Ibid, Miller, Newsweek

9) T. D. Jakes, *Reposition Yourself – Living Life Without Limits.* (New York: Atria Books, 2007), pg. 47

10) John C. Maxwell, "Revelation—The Revealing of Jesus to the World," *The Maxwell Leadership Bible.* (Nashville: Thomas Nelson Publishers, 2002), pg. 1557

11) Dr. Benjamin Mays, God's Minute, the world renown educator's classic poem

12) Going To Heaven, Old Negro Spiritual

13) St. Francis of Assisi concerning being an instrument of peace

14) Holy, Holy, Holy written by Reginald Heber (1783-1826)

15) Twila Paris, Lamb of God, 1985 EMI Christian Music Mountain Spring Music Straightway Music

16) Hallelujah, by George Frideric Händel, public domain.

17) Kendall H. Easley, *Holman New Testament Commentary, Revelation*, Max Anders, General Editor, (Nashville: Holman Reference, 1998), pg. 245

18) Battle Hymn of the Republic, Julia Ward Howe

19) James Montgomery, Prayer Is The Soul's Desire, 1818

20) Dr. Frank M. Reid, III, *Restoring The House of God – A Plea for Radical Reformation*, (Shippensburg, PA: Treasure House, 2000), pg. 118

21) Richard Bauckham, "Understanding Revelation," *Zondervan Handbook to the Bible*, (Grand Rapids, MI: Zondervan Publishing House) pg. 771

22) God In The Ghetto, William A. Jones, Jr., Progressive Baptist Publishing House, Elgin, IL, pg. 61

23) Be At The Meeting, classic gospel quartet song made famous by the Sensational Nightingales.

24) Heav'n, Heav'n, Negro Spiritual

25) Josh McDowell concerning the deity of Jesus Christ

26) Rosa Parks, The Mother of the Civil Rights Movement, concerning her historic act of civil disobedience.

27) Rosa Parks, The Mother of the Civil Rights Movement, concerning her life and legacy.

28) Rosa Parks, The Mother of the Civil Rights Movement, concerning overcoming fear.

29) Rosa Parks, Mother of the Civil Rights Movement, Memories

30) Sit Down Servant, Negro Spiritual

31) The Measure of a Man: by Martin Luther King Jr., Sermon- The Dimensions of a Complete Life, Publisher: Augsburg Fortress Publishers

32) Velma Maia Thomas, No Man Can Hinder Me: The Journey from Slavery to Emancipation through Song (New York: Crown Publishers, 2001), pg. 14

33) Every Time I Feel The Spirit, Negro Spiritual

34) Steal Away, Negro Spiritual

35) Let My People Go, Negro Spiritual

36) Warren W. Wiersbe, *With the Word – The Chapter-by-Chapter Handbook*, (Nashville: Thomas Nelson Publishers, 1991), pg. 849

37) We Shall Overcome, Anthem of the Civil Rights Movement

38) Excerpted from "The Drum Major Instinct", a sermon by Rev. Martin Luther King, Jr., 1968. A Knock At Midnight: Inspiration from the Great Sermons of Reverend Martin Luther King, Jr.

39) Rev. Dr. Martin Luther King, Jr., Speech in Detroit, Michigan, 1963

40) Great Day, Negro Spiritual

41) Listen To The Angels Shouting, Negro Spiritual

42) Oh Freedom, Negro Spiritual

43) Walk In Jerusalem Just Like John, Negro Spiritual

44) Ibid, Martin Luther King Jr.

45) The New York Times, Lives Lived Well And the Lessons That They Teach, A MINISTER IN MANY PULPITS, December 26, 1999

46) Michael Slater, Becoming A Stretcher Bearer – Lifting One Another in Times of Need with the Gifts of Encouragement and Support, Regal Books, Ventura, California, 1985, 1989, pg. 46

47) A Charge To Keep I Have, Charles Wesley, *Short Hymns on Select Passages of Holy Scripture*, 1762. *Music:* Boylston, Lowell Mason, *The Choir, or Union Collection of Church Music*, 1832

48) General George S. Patton concerning overcoming and high goals

49) Father, I Stretch My Hands to Thee—Words: Charles Wesley, A Collection of Songs and Hymns, 1741. Music: Naomi, Hans G. Nägeli, arranged by Lowell Mason, 1836.

50) Dietrich Bonhoeffer, German Theologian and Lutheran Pastor, The Cost of Discipleship, 1937

51) Stormie Omartian, *Seven Prayers That Will Change Your Life Forever*, (Nashville: J.Countryman, a division of Thomas Nelson, Inc., 2006), pg. 12

ABOUT THE AUTHOR

Pastor **Arthur L. Mackey Jr.** of the Mount Sinai Baptist Church Cathedral in Roosevelt, New York, is an anointed preacher and teacher committed to reaching the world with the Gospel of Jesus Christ. He is married to the lovely Brenda Jackson Mackey. They have three children: Yolanda, Jordan, and Faith. Pastor Mackey is also the founder and president of Arthur Mackey Ministries, Vision of Victory Ministries, and Mackey Productions.

In addition to his church and media ministries, Pastor Mackey is also the author of several books, including: *The Biblical Principles of Success; Walking Through the Doorways of Destiny; Inner Healing for Men; Inner Healing for Women;* and *Real Revival.* He has also written many worship songs, including: "Source of Inner Healing," "Accepted in the Beloved," "Revive Thy Work," and "Break Forth".

A graduate of Virginia Union University in Richmond, Virginia, where he majored in Religion and Philosophy, Pastor

Mackey is called of God to ministry in order that many would experience true deliverance, inner healing and real revival.

THE SINNER'S PRAYER

The First Step toward True Success

Father God, in the mighty, marvelous, and matchless name of Jesus, I come crying before your eternal throne of grace, realizing that the place where I am right now has become my mourner's bench of sorrow and repentance.

Heavenly Father, I am asking You to forgive me of all my sins, faults, lies, misdirected desires, and shortcomings. Today, I accept as an undeniable fact, that more than two thousand years ago on Calvary's old rugged cross, Jesus Christ of Nazareth washed away my sins as far as the east is from the west. That is an infinite line that never stops. That is how far my personal, public, and private sins have been thrown away. They now have been cast down into the sea of forgetfulness! I personally proclaim at this very moment that Jesus Christ lived, died, and rose from the dead that I might receive true salvation. Today, I accept, confess, and believe deeply within that Jesus

Christ is the liberating Lord of my life and the satisfying Savior of my soul.

Now, Lord, I ask You to lead, guide, and direct me through the Holy Spirit from one degree of grace unto another. While I am on this journey of new growth, learning, and Christian development, teach me, Heavenly Master, how to walk day by day in the footsteps of Your Son, Jesus Christ. Amen.

Name: _____

Date: _____

Real Revival
by <u>Arthur L. Mackey Jr.</u> / Paperback / ISBN
075960584X

Inner Healing for Men
by <u>Arthur L. Mackey Jr.</u> / Paperback / ISBN
1562291238

Inner Healing for Women
by <u>Arthur L. Mackey Jr.</u> / Paperback / ISBN
1562291246

Walking Through the Doorways of Destiny
by <u>Arthur L. Mackey Jr.</u> / Paperback / ISBN
1562294555

Revival in the Valley of Dry Bones
by <u>Arthur L. Mackey Jr.</u> / Paperback / ISBN
1597811564

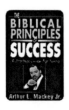

The Biblical Principles of Success by
<u>Arthur L. Mackey Jr.</u> / Paperback / ISBN-10:
1562294547

WRITE THE AUTHOR

PASTOR ARTHUR L. MACKEY JR.
MT. SINAI BAPTIST CHURCH
CATHEDRAL
243 REV. DR. ARTHUR L. MACKEY SR. AVE.
ROOSEVELT, NEW YORK 11575
(516) 868-0076

Notes For The Overcomer

9 780615 190778